SELF-HARM

By Stephanie Mialki

Portions of this book originally appeared in *Self-Injury* by Toney Allman.

LUCENT PRESS

Published in 2017 by
Lucent Press, an Imprint of Greenhaven Publishing, LLC
353 3rd Avenue
Suite 255
New York, NY 10010

Designer: Andrea Davison-Bartolotta
Editor: Jennifer Lombardo

Cataloging-in-Publication Data

Names: Mialki, Stephanie.
Title: Self-harm / Stephanie Mialki.
Description: New York : Lucent Press, 2017. | Series: Hot topics | Includes index.
Identifiers: ISBN 9781534560178 (library bound) | ISBN 9781534560185 (ebook)
Subjects: LCSH: Self-mutilation in adolescence–Juvenile literature. | Self-injurious behavior-
-Juvenile literature. | Cutting (Self-mutilation)–Juvenile literature.
Classification: LCC RJ506.S44 M53 2017 | DDC 616.85'82–dc23

Printed in the United States of America

CPSIA compliance information: Batch #CW17KL: For further information contact Greenhaven Publishing LLC, New York,
New York at 1-844-317-7404.

Please visit our website, www.greenhavenpublishing.com. For a free color catalog of all our
high-quality books, call toll free 1-844-317-7404 or fax 1-844-317-7405.

CONTENTS

Adolescence is a time when many people begin to take notice of the world around them. News channels, blogs, and talk radio shows are constantly promoting one view or another; very few are unbiased. Young people also hear conflicting information from parents, friends, teachers, and acquaintances. Often, they will hear only one side of an issue or be given flawed information. People who are trying to support a particular viewpoint may cite inaccurate facts and statistics on their blogs, and news programs present many conflicting views of important issues in our society. In a world where it seems everyone has a platform to share their thoughts, it can be difficult to find unbiased, accurate information about important issues.

It is not only facts that are important. In blog posts, in comments on online videos, and on talk shows, people will share opinions that are not necessarily true or false, but can still have a strong impact. For example, many young people struggle with their body image. Seeing or hearing negative comments about particular body types online can have a huge effect on the way someone views himself or herself and may lead to depression and anxiety. Although it is important not to keep information hidden from young people under the guise of protecting them, it is equally important to offer encouragement on issues that affect their mental health.

The titles in the Hot Topics series provide readers with different viewpoints on important issues in today's society. Many of these issues, such as teen pregnancy and Internet safety, are of immediate concern to young people. This series aims to give readers factual context on these crucial topics in a way that lets them form their own opinions. The facts presented throughout also serve to empower readers to help themselves or support people they know who are struggling with many of the challenges adolescents face today. Although negative viewpoints are not ignored or downplayed, this series allows young people to see that the challenges they face are not insurmountable. Eating disorders can be overcome, the Internet can be navigated safely, and pregnant teens do not have to feel hopeless.

Quotes encompassing all viewpoints are presented and cited so readers can trace them back to their original source, verifying for themselves whether the information comes from a reputable place. Additional books and websites are listed, giving readers a starting point from which to continue their own research. Chapter questions encourage discussion, allowing young people to hear and understand their classmates' points of view as they further solidify their own. Full-color photographs and enlightening charts provide a deeper understanding of the topics at hand. All of these features augment the informative text, helping young people understand the world they live in and formulate their own opinions concerning the best way they can improve it.

A Growing Epidemic.

For many, the idea of self-injury can conjure up a variety of images. "Self-injury" is an all-encompassing term to describe many different types of injuries that result from deliberately wounding oneself, including cutting, burning, hitting, and scraping. It is a way for people to cope with serious psychological distress.

As the numbers of reported self-injurious behaviors continue to rise (especially in young people), researchers and experts worldwide look to find the cause out of concern for the well-being of those affected. Self-injury can cause permanent physical damage, especially when the injurious behavior accidentally or purposefully goes too far. The results can be disastrous; from a cut too deep to a burn too severe, the injuries can turn into deep wound infections, permanent nerve damage, or even lifelong disability or death.

The increase in occurrences means more people than ever are studying this topic. Society has become more aware of self-injury and its dangers, which has made teachers and parents especially concerned. Their struggle to fully understand self-injury is made more difficult by the fact that there are many myths and misunderstandings surrounding the topic. Even worse, those who suffer continue to live in secret shame while remaining convinced that they must continue their self-injurious habits in order to survive and cope with overwhelming emotional distress.

Those who suffer from their self-injurious behaviors fall into several different categories. Many wish to be left alone so they can continue to harm themselves, while others may wish they could stop. What is most important is that all wish to be treated with compassion and respect. Reactions of fear, horror, and disgust serve to only worsen the situation and prolong the suffering. The labels of attention-seeking, manipulative, suicidal, or even crazy are all inaccurate and only dampen the efforts of researchers, experts, friends, and family.

Education is the key to the continued fight against self-injury. The Self Injury Foundation is dedicated to doing just that: educating everyone about self-harm, as well as standing as a beacon to those who suffer and do not know how to cope any other way. The organization says that its mission is "to provide funding for research, advocacy support and education for self-injurers, their loved ones and the professionals who work with them. We are dedicated to providing the most up to date information and resources available on self-injury."[1]

March 1 is Self-Injury Awareness Day. Many people wear orange ribbons on that day to raise awareness about self-harm.

However, not everyone agrees on the need to educate people about self-harm. On one hand, the American Self-Harm Information Clearinghouse stands firm in its belief that education creates a reduction in the number of people who self-injure, as well as a corresponding increase in compassion for self-injurers. The organization subscribes to the theory that self-injury is the result of an overwhelming need to relieve tension and stress for a variety of psychological, biological, and environmental reasons.

In contrast, critics point to peer pressure as a possible reason for self-harm incidence. This "learned action" approach is based on the idea that self-injurious behavior in young people can be adopted as a learned action through outlets such as the Internet, media, or through imitation of others. Even educational programs can ignite the spark of self-injurious ideas, turning it from thought to action.

Thus, many see the increase in self-injury awareness as potentially causing a cycle of self-harm. Sociologist Sarah Hodgson argues that the chances of people beginning to self-injure "increase as information on self-injury is becoming more widely available."[2] In response, some experts view the widespread education about self-injury as potentially dangerous, especially to young adults, who are most affected and possibly most prone to the behavior. However, self-injury can affect people of all socioeconomic statuses, ages, and genders. While some are "functioning"—that is, able to manage many of life's tasks such as demanding jobs and home lives—others may find all aspects of life suffering from the self-injurious behavior.

Due to this incredible diversity in those affected, there is no single solution to self-injury. Experts cannot offer simple answers about who sufferers are, why they self-harm, or how to help them choose not to self-injure. However, there is one thing experts agree on, and that is the self-destruction of the habit and the underlying emotional issues in need of resolution.

While each individual is different, their self-injurious behaviors may be overcome depending on their willingness and readiness to work with a therapist. Counselor, writer, and advocate Deb Martinson advises self-injurers, "Deciding to stop self-injury is a very personal decision. You may have to consider it for a long time before you decide that you're ready to commit to a life without scars and bruises."[3] Recovery can be difficult and sometimes emotionally painful, but the time and effort are well worth it. Many sufferers confirm that they finally stopped injuring themselves when they learned how to love themselves again.

CHAPTER 1

Intentional
Personal Harm

The reasons for self-harm vary from person to person, but in almost all cases, the emotions a sufferer feels include rejection, shame, and disgust with themselves. For example, one 14-year-old named Samantha began to harm herself because she constantly believed that her appearance and weight fell short of her ideal model: her mother. These insecurities began to trickle through to how she viewed herself as a worthwhile person.

As a result, Samantha began to cut herself. Her forearms were the target of the injuries; she hid the cuts and scars by covering her arms with a long-sleeved shirt even in the heat of

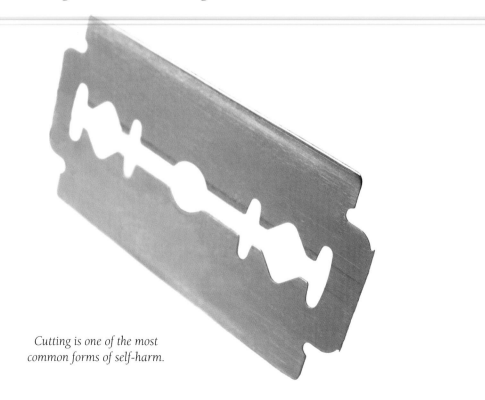

Cutting is one of the most common forms of self-harm.

summer. She explained, "When things are going well for me, I do not cut myself, but when I start to feel worried about my body, I want to punish myself for how I look."[4]

In another circumstance, 17-year-old Jack also cut his arms to cope with the overwhelming stresses in his life. In order to deal with his anger and emotional pain, Jack said, "Sometimes I feel numb, and inflicting pain is the only way I truly feel something."[5]

Unlike Samantha and Jack, Chrissie, a woman in her late 20s, could not hide her injuries from the world. One of her first experiences was in early childhood, when she rubbed a pencil eraser on her skin until she bled. As she grew, her injurious behaviors became more destructive. In adulthood, Chrissie began using knives and razor blades to cut all over her body. In some instances, the injuries were so bad that she needed hundreds of stitches.

Luke, a middle-aged man, found many methods of self-injury; he cut himself, burned himself, and poured acid on his hands. He explained how he developed a tolerance to the pain: "It's like a drug. Sometimes, I don't realize I'm even doing it."[6]

The Basics of Self-Injury

Samantha, Jack, Chrissie, and Luke are of different ages, use different tactics, experience different feelings, and explain their behaviors in different ways, but they all have one thing in common—they use self-injury to cope with their lives and emotions. Self-harm may also be called self-injury or self-mutilation, but it is officially called non-suicidal self-injury (NSSI). In their book *Self-Injury in Youth: The Essential Guide to Assessment and Intervention*, researchers Mary K. Nixon and Nancy L. Heath explain, "It can be defined as purposely inflicting injury that results in immediate tissue damage, done without suicidal intent and not socially sanctioned within one's culture nor for display … NSSI includes, but is not limited to, cutting, pin-scratching, carving, burning, and self-hitting."[7]

The "non-suicidal" part of the term is important. At one time, medical experts lumped self-injury together with suicide

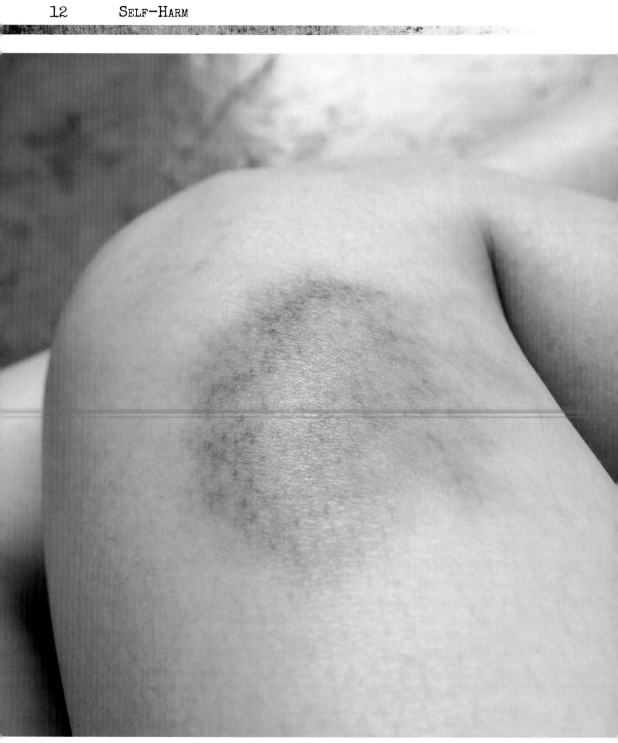

One form of self-harm is when people hit themselves hard enough to leave bruises.

attempts and labeled them as "parasuicide"—near or resembling suicide. Today, however, most knowledgeable people reject that definition. Even people like Chrissie who injure themselves severely, say experts, are not trying to commit suicide nor are they making suicidal gestures. They do not self-injure because they want to die. They have an emotional problem or psychological disorder that causes them to attack their skin and the tissue beneath the skin in a way that causes injury, bleeding, wounds, or marks. The attack is a coping mechanism and a way to relieve negative or unpleasant emotions, not an effort to disable or kill themselves, although between 40 and 80 percent of self-injurers do have suicidal ideations (thoughts). The difference is that they are not using their self-harming behaviors to follow through on those ideations; they think about suicide but do not attempt it in most cases. Less than half (about 30 percent) of teenagers who injure themselves have also attempted suicide at one point in their lives.

A Dangerous Coping Mechanism

Some experts, such as social worker Elana Premack Sandler, say that the goal of NSSI is not even to permanently change or scar the body, although scars are the usual outcome. Actually, NSSI is motivated by an attempt to deal with life, rather than to escape life. In a strange way, it is an attempt to save oneself—to prevent the misery and depression that might lead to suicide—rather than an attempt to destroy oneself. For example, Sandler described one teenage girl whose parents hospitalized her when they discovered that she was cutting herself. In the hospital, the girl was prevented by staff members from cutting herself, so she did attempt suicide. Sandler said, "I can't help but think about how that experience [the withdrawal of her coping tool] might have contributed to her suicide attempt."[8] Without the alternative of self-injury, the girl lapsed into hopelessness and wanted to die.

Medical doctors, psychologists, social workers, and other experts do not always agree about the definition of self-injury, but Sandler and most others see a big difference between self-injury and suicide attempts. In addition, Sandler and most others agree with Nixon and Heath in describing self-injury as a private activity, not a public one. Therefore, it is not often a bid for attention. Although tattoos and body piercings involve changes to the body by means of sharp objects, the end results of those activities are meant to be seen. In contrast, self-injurers typically try to hide the evidence of their self-harm. This means that they rarely cut, burn, or harm themselves in the presence of other people. Psychologist Tracy Alderman explained:

> Most people who get tattooed and/or pierced are proud of their new decorations. They want to show others their ink, their studs, their plugs. They want to tell the story of the pain, the fear, the experience. In contrast, those who hurt themselves generally don't tell anyone about it. Self-injurers go to great lengths to cover and disguise their wounds and scars. Self-injurers are not proud of their new decorations.[9]

Modern Diagnosis

Most clinicians (health professionals who work with and treat patients) consider NSSI an associated feature of other disorders, such as anxiety, depression, eating disorders, or post-traumatic stress disorder (PTSD). It is not generally considered a mental illness in and of itself. In the United States, clinicians use the standards and criteria set out by the American Psychiatric Association (APA) to diagnose psychological syndromes and problems. The symptoms of syndromes are described in a manual called the *Diagnostic and Statistical Manual of Mental Disorders, 5th Edition (DSM-5)*. Using the *DSM-5*, clinicians generally diagnose a person who self-injures as having one of the psychological disorders described in the manual. In this system, self-injury is just one symptom of another psychological disorder, but it does have its own criteria for diagnosis. These include the following:

- *The act is not socially acceptable.*
- *The act or its consequence can cause significant distress to the individual's daily life.*
- *The act is not taking place during psychotic episodes, delirium, substance intoxication, or substance withdrawal. It also cannot be explained by another medical condition.*

Although tattoos and piercings hurt, they are different from self-injury in that they are meant to be seen, while self-injurers typically keep scars and wounds covered.

- *The individual engages in self-injury expecting:*
  - » *[To] get relief from a negative emotion*
  - » *To deal with a personal issue*
  - » *To create a positive feeling*
- *The self-injury is associated with one of the following:*
  - » *The individual experienced negative feelings right before committing the act.*
  - » *Right before self-injury, the individual was preoccupied with the planned act.*
  - » *The individual thinks a lot about self-injury even if [the] act does not take place.*[10]

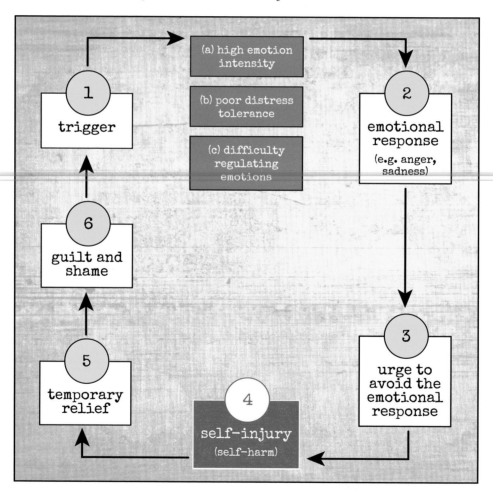

The negative emotions associated with NSSI can keep the cycle going, as this chart shows, based on information from Australia's Mental Health Professional Online Development website.

The *DSM-5* does include a disorder called non-suicidal self-injury disorder (NSSID), which is different from NSSI because it classifies self-injury as its own disorder, rather than an associated feature of another disorder. However, many clinicians do not agree with this inclusion. Psychiatrist Shirah Vollmer said:

> *The act of cutting does not communicate the essence of the patient's struggle, only that some sort of struggle is going on. This is the difference between a symptom and a diagnosis. A diagnosis is an answer and a symptom starts the questioning. Once a diagnosis is made, questioning often stops, and treatment begins. With NSSID, this should start the inquiry, and not lead to quick labeling and a certainty of a mental illness which underlies the behavior. Mental distress does not equal mental illness.*[11]

Psychological Correlation with Borderline Personality Disorder

One of the most common diagnoses for people who self-injure is called borderline personality disorder (BPD). The major characteristic of this disorder is instability. People with BPD do not have stable relationships with other people. They do not have stable emotions, either, and may become very angry, panicky, or despairing when other people seem to "let them down" or not care enough about them. Borderline personality disorder often means acting on emotional impulse rather than thinking things through. It means having mood swings or intense emotions that can change quickly—for example, from being extremely happy to being terribly anxious or depressed. People with BPD also have a poor self-image; they report feeling empty and worthless. They are afraid of losing loved ones, fear being rejected or unloved, and may frantically try to prevent other people from abandoning them, sometimes for no good reason.

The *DSM-5* lists several symptoms of BPD, one of which is taking risks without concern for the consequences. This can include things such as online gambling, reckless driving, and self-harm. A person who self-injures and shows signs of instability may be diagnosed with BPD.

Celebrities and Self-Harm

Mental and emotional issues can affect anyone, even people whose lives appear to be perfect. Many celebrities have spoken out about their struggles with issues such as eating disorders, depression, anxiety, and self-harm. Some of them still face these issues; others dealt with them when they were younger, but still remember the pain of those struggles. Johnny Depp has confirmed that some of his scars came from self-harm when he was a teenager; Russell Brand cut himself when he was younger, possibly as a result of his manic depression and bipolar disorder; and Demi Lovato has turned her history of self-harm into a campaign to help others who suffer from the same issues. In an MTV special called *Stay Strong*, Lovato opened up about her struggle to overcome her self-harming behaviors and eating disorder and encouraged fellow sufferers to seek help.

Demi Lovato has been outspoken about how important it is for people to seek help when they need it.

Other Psychological Correlations

People who self-injure might be diagnosed as having mood disorders instead of BPD. Mood disorders are psychological disorders that affect a person's mood and include depression and bipolar disorder. Depression is characterized by constant sadness, lack of energy, feelings of hopelessness and worthlessness, and thoughts of suicide. It is believed to be caused by an imbalance of chemicals in the brain. Bipolar disorder is characterized by moods that swing between the extremes of depression and mania, or excited, energetic thoughts and feelings. Like depression, it is thought to be related to changes in the normal chemicals in the brain. Mood disorders are listed in *DSM-5* and diagnosed according to lists of symptoms. When a person who self-injures also reports depression, extreme mood swings, or suicidal thoughts, a clinician might diagnose a mood disorder. The mood disorder is assumed to be causing the associated feature of self-harm.

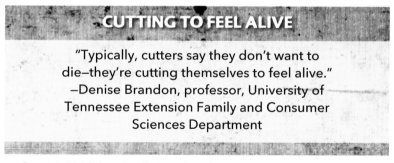

CUTTING TO FEEL ALIVE

"Typically, cutters say they don't want to die—they're cutting themselves to feel alive."
—Denise Brandon, professor, University of Tennessee Extension Family and Consumer Sciences Department

Quoted in Kristi Nelson, *Knoxville News Sentinel*, June 1, 2010. www.knoxnews.com/news/local/woman-draws-on-her-own-experience-with-self-injury-to-help-others-ep-408340721-358701351.html.

Another psychological disorder associated with brain chemical imbalances is called obsessive-compulsive disorder (OCD). OCD is marked by repeated and long-lasting thoughts and worries that will not go away. It is also characterized by the need, or compulsion, to repeat certain activities, such as constant hand-washing, so as to ward off some terrible feeling or disaster; the compulsion may be so overwhelming that the person has little time to engage in normal activities. Sometimes, people with OCD may compulsively harm themselves. The self-injury generally takes the form of hair pulling (from the head, body, eyelashes, or eyebrows) or constant picking or scratching at the skin. If a person who self-injures does so compulsively and feels that he or she must pull out hair or damage skin to prevent something terrible from happening, that person may be diagnosed with OCD.

Implications of Anxiety and Trauma

DSM-5 also lists a large category of anxiety disorders, and sometimes people who self-injure are diagnosed with an anxiety disorder. Since people who self-injure may do so to relieve stress or to calm themselves, some clinicians believe that self-injury can arise from serious, prolonged anxiety and tension. The self-injury is a symptom of the anxiety disorder and is used to decrease anxiousness, tension, and overwhelming feelings of panic and worry.

Many experts who study or treat self-injury see the disorder—at least sometimes—as a symptom of PTSD. This diagnosis suggests that the cause of self-injury is a trauma that the person has undergone in the past. A trauma is any overwhelming event that leaves a person feeling powerless, helpless, or in danger. Some examples of traumas include living through a severe earthquake, becoming a prisoner of war, being raped or assaulted, or being physically abused as a child. These experiences can be so emotionally upsetting that they are difficult to accept or adjust to, even when the traumatic event is over. Some scientists suggest that the trauma may even affect the brain by causing a chemical imbalance. People with PTSD may have a range of symptoms that include fear, trouble sleeping, stress, anxiety, anger, abusing drugs or alcohol to numb their feelings, and depression. People who self-injure may be diagnosed with PTSD if they are coping with their trauma by hurting themselves to deal with and soothe their feelings.

Failure to Diagnose

According to diagnostic standards today, people may self-injure as a result of several different psychological disorders.

*Those returning from war are one of several groups at risk for PTSD, which
increases chances of self-injurious behaviors.*

Incarceration and Self-Injury

The incidence of self-injury in prison populations is known to be quite high. A survey of prisoners in the United Kingdom found that approximately 30 percent of female prisoners and 6 percent of male prisoners injured themselves. The younger the inmates were, the more likely they were to experiment with self-injury.

In the United States, approximately 2 to 4 percent of all inmates are known to self-injure, and according to one study, 53 percent of them did so after being placed in solitary confinement. Prisoners most often cut themselves with sharp objects, swallow dangerous objects, bang their heads against walls, or open old wounds. According to Lorry Schoenly, a correctional system nurse, prison staff generally believe that prisoners self-injure out of boredom or to get attention. She says, however, that the self-injury is "motivated by a 'coping deficit' when dealing with feelings of depression or powerlessness."[1]

In prison, people are indeed powerless, and they often suffer from psychological disorders. The research organization Urban Institute reported in 2015 that "56 percent of state prisoners [and] 45 percent of federal prisoners"[2] suffer from serious mental illnesses such as schizophrenia, bipolar disorder, or depression. People in prison have little independence and often are allowed few supportive social contacts. Experts believe that both the prison environment and previous psychological disorders play a role in increasing the risk of self-injury among prisoners.

1.   Lorry Schoenly, "I'm Gonna Hurt Myself," *Correctional Nurse*, February 8, 2010. lorryschoenly.wordpress.com/tag/self-injury-behavior.

2.   KiDeuk Kim, Miriam Becker-Cohen, and Maria Serakos, "The Processing and Treatment of Mentally Ill Persons in the Criminal Justice System," Urban Institute, March 2015. www.urban.org/research/publication/processing-and-treatment-mentally-ill-persons-criminal-justice-system/view/full_report.

Incarceration seems to have a correlation with self-injury.

Self-injury is not its own disorder and often cannot even be diagnosed unless the self-injurer tells a clinician about the problem. As a secretive behavior, it can go undiagnosed for years. Until 2013, when the *DSM-5* replaced the previous version, there was not even a real set of criteria for diagnosis. This situation was disturbing to many self-injury researchers and clinicians. They wanted to agree on a better definition of self-injury and educate the public and professionals about the importance of identifying and helping self-injurers. They campaigned to have diagnostic criteria included in the *DSM-5* in order to accomplish those goals.

According to the mental health advocacy organization National Alliance on Mental Illness (NAMI), 75 percent of people who are diagnosed with BPD self-injure. However, some experts wonder if these people truly have BPD or if they are merely diagnosed with BPD because they injure themselves. In 1997, for instance, psychologist S. Herpertz and his colleagues studied people who self-injure and discovered that only 48 percent of them met the criteria for having BPD. When the scientists excluded the symptom of self-injury, they reported that only 28 percent of self-injurers met the other criteria for BPD. Some scientists have argued that too many

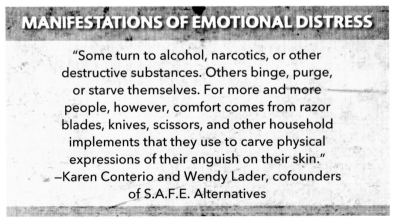

MANIFESTATIONS OF EMOTIONAL DISTRESS

"Some turn to alcohol, narcotics, or other destructive substances. Others binge, purge, or starve themselves. For more and more people, however, comfort comes from razor blades, knives, scissors, and other household implements that they use to carve physical expressions of their anguish on their skin."
—Karen Conterio and Wendy Lader, cofounders of S.A.F.E. Alternatives

Karen Conterio and Wendy Lader, *Bodily Harm*. New York, NY: Hyperion, 1998, p. 16.

clinicians simply diagnose BPD whenever they discover that a person self-injures.

Some clinicians reject the BPD diagnosis and instead diagnose an impulse control disorder (ICD). Like mood disorders, ICD refers to a type of disorder rather than one specific one. Eating disorders, compulsive gambling, kleptomania (compulsive stealing), and alcohol addiction are all considered impulse disorders because the sufferer is unable to resist hurting themselves or others. This disorder is used as a diagnosis for anyone who has strong impulses or temptations that are hard to resist. The person diagnosed with this disorder feels great tension when trying to resist the temptation and then experiences relief after giving in to it.

The Profile of Self-Injurers

Accurate diagnosis and understanding of self-injury is important to medical and psychological professionals today because self-injury seems to be a growing problem around the world. In 2010, in the *Journal of the American Board of Family Medicine*, psychologist Patrick Kerr and his team reported "an increasing prevalence of self-injury, especially among adolescents [teens] and young adults."[12] This trend has continued through the present day. No one knows why self-injury might be increasing, but today's experts say that anywhere from 4 to 30 percent of teens have reported self-injurious behaviors. Exact numbers are very difficult to find because self-injurers try so hard to keep their activities secret. In the United States, approximately 1 to 4 percent of adults self-injure. Among college students, the rate of self-injury is reported to be between 17 to 35 percent.

Self-injury seems to begin in youth. Most people start to self-injure between the ages of 13 and 15. Experts used to believe that girls and women were much more likely to self-injure than boys and men, but Kerr and his team say that current research shows that males and females are equally likely to self-injure. Men are more likely to make their injuries large and noticeable, typically cutting or burning places such as their chest or upper arms; women are more likely to keep their injuries small and hidden, in places such as the inner thighs. In Western society, it is sometimes seen as acceptable for men to deal with anger or frustration by using violence toward themselves, others, or inanimate objects. Women, on the other hand, are expected to keep displays of emotion hidden. People of both sexes may hide their self-harm behaviors, however, out of fear of being dismissed as only doing it for attention. In other words, they fear that people will assume they are putting on an act rather than genuinely needing help. This can make it difficult for them to come forward and tell people what is going on, which means many self-injurers do not get the psychiatric help they need.

The United States is not the only country where people harm themselves. In Canada, a 2008 study found that 16.9 percent of teens had harmed themselves. According to the British National Self Harm Network (NSHN), the United Kingdom has one of the worst problems with self-injury throughout Europe. The rate is estimated to be 400 out of every 100,000 people. In 2008, child psychologist Nicola Madge conducted a study of teens in 7 different European countries that showed that 3 in 10 girls and 1 in 10 boys had either harmed themselves or thought of harming themselves during the past year. In this study, cutting was the most common form of self-injury, and about 25 percent of the young people interviewed had successfully hidden their self-injury from everyone. Madge concluded that statistics about self-injury probably do not reveal the extent of the disorder among European youth. She said, "This research shows that self-harm is an international, widespread yet often hidden problem."[13]

Statistics and information about self-injury are not available in many parts of the world, but most experts believe that the disorder is common everywhere, although different methods of harm may be used in different places. In Pakistan, for example, self-poisoning is often preferred and can result in death, even though suicide is not the person's intention. Experts say that self-injurers who survive are not often reported to medical professionals because attempted suicide is against the law in Pakistan and is considered a sin in the Muslim religion. British physician and poisons expert Michael Eddleston called self-harm "an overlooked tragedy in the developing world."[14] In Sri Lanka, for instance, poison is also a common means of self-harm, and, as a

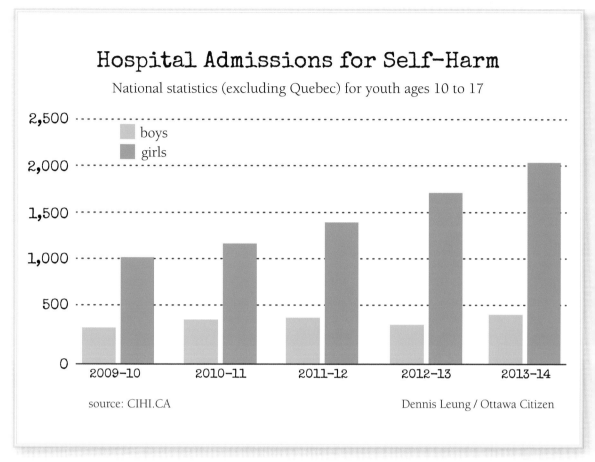

Hospital Admissions for Self-Harm

National statistics (excluding Quebec) for youth ages 10 to 17

- boys
- girls

source: CIHI.CA   Dennis Leung / Ottawa Citizen

The United States does not track self-harm rates, but Canada shows an increase in incidents of self-harm for both boys and girls since 2009.

result, Sri Lanka, Eddleston says, has a very high suicide rate (40 per 100,000 people per year) compared with the British suicide rate (11 per 100,000 people). Eddleston explained that most of the young people who die from self-poisoning do not mean to kill themselves. They are trying to cope with stress or difficult problems by means of self-injury and die accidentally.

Understanding Self-Injury Today

The goal of NSSI may not be death or permanent disability, yet that is a real risk run by people who repeatedly self-injure, no

matter what the method. Self-injury is dangerous, and it can
be hard to understand as a method of coping. Why do people
cut or burn or poison themselves? Just as experts try to accurately define and diagnose self-injury, they also try to identify
the causes of self-injury and explain how some people develop
the strong need to hurt themselves.

CHAPTER 2

Reasons for Self-Injury

Self-injury has long been known as a coping mechanism for sufferers to deal with severe emotional distress. The real cause for this repetitive, non-suicidal destruction has yet to be fully revealed.

Why do some people choose self-injury to cope? Why do some people consider injuring themselves a valid way to deal with negative thoughts and feelings? These important questions have been discussed by experts, but opinions among these experts vary. Many agree that those who self-harm do so for a variety of reasons, although these reasons are still not well understood. The consensus remains, though, that self-injury seems to be a way for some to deal with intense feelings of extreme emotional distress and pain.

Severe Emotional Distress

Many people turn to injuring themselves when they feel strong emotions that they have no good way of dealing with. Some of these emotions include jealousy, anger, sadness, and self-disgust. They may feel rejected or unloved by friends and family; they may also feel overwhelmed and out of control of their lives. Others may feel emotionally numb and hurt themselves because they believe the pain is better than the numbness.

Self-injury treatment experts Karen Conterio, an alcohol and addictions counselor, and Wendy Lader, a clinical psychologist, say that the purposes behind self-injury can be divided into two major categories. The first is "analgesic or palliative,"[15] which means eliminating or reducing pain. The second is "communicative."[16] By Conterio and Lader's definition, this means expressing and acting out emotional pain, either to oneself or to others as a cry for help.

Some people use their self-injury to feel better about themselves; it is a soothing action for them. Others may be

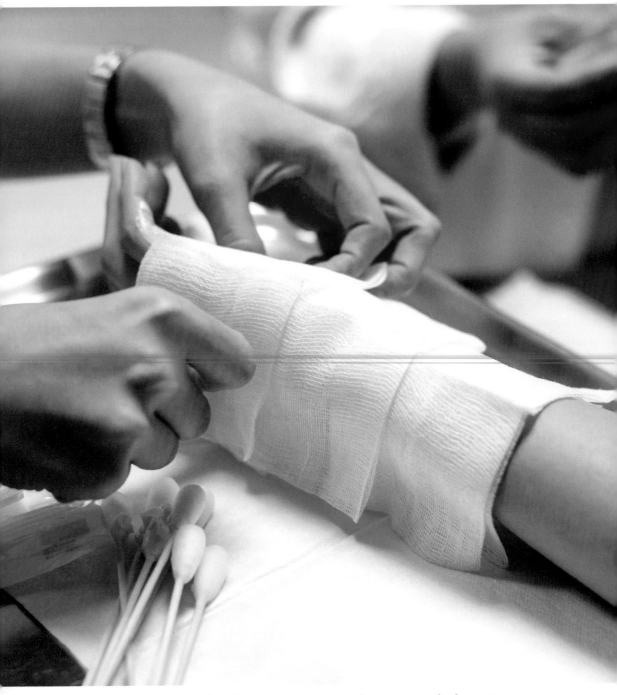

Sometimes, self-inflicted injuries are severe enough to require medical attention.

communicating how worthless they feel or that they think they deserve to be punished. Conterio and Lader described Jared T., who calls his self-injury "the tangible face to my intangible pain—see my pain!" Jared thinks, "I'll show them just how worthless I am, and how much I hurt."[17] Other self-injurers may believe that bleeding from injuries cleanses them of the emotional poison inside them or is a way to punish themselves for things they did wrong, whether real or imagined. However, Conterio and Lader explain that self-injurers generally cannot describe what about them is so sinful or bad. Even when self-injurers keep their actions hidden, they may be secretly wishing that someone would see their pain and care enough to want to save them from the injuries and reassure them that they are good and worthwhile. However, most of the time, explain Conterio, Lader, and other experts in the self-harm field, self-injurers feel so helpless, worthless, and ashamed of who they are that they cannot believe the good things others say about them.

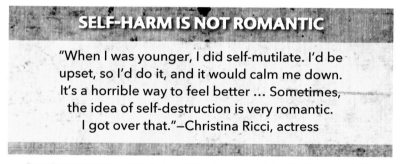

SELF-HARM IS NOT ROMANTIC

"When I was younger, I did self-mutilate. I'd be upset, so I'd do it, and it would calm me down. It's a horrible way to feel better … Sometimes, the idea of self-destruction is very romantic. I got over that."–Christina Ricci, actress

Quoted in Jamie Diamond, "Okay, She's Not All Sweetness and Light, but Who Wants Her to Be?" *Mademoiselle*, 1999. www.christina-ricci.com/press-archive/mademoiselle-1999.

Implications of Childhood Trauma

How can people come to feel so bad about themselves that they need to hurt and injure themselves? One theory proposed by self-injury researchers and clinicians is abuse or trauma during childhood. Conterio says that in surveys, about half of all people who self-injure report being abused as children. In some studies, those numbers are even more dramatic. For instance, the National Center for PTSD found that 93 percent of one group of self-injurers reported childhood abuse. Armando Favazza, who wrote the first professional book on self-harm, also said that childhood abuse is commonly linked with self-injury and eating disorders (another way of harming oneself).

Clinicians who treat self-injurers report the same connection with early abuse. Childhood abuse can cause a psychological problem called dissociation, a kind of psychological defense against extreme trauma in which people disconnect from their emotions and experiences. They "zone out" to protect themselves and are numb to emotional or physical pain. They feel as if the trauma is happening to someone else or as if they are removed from their bodies. Dissociation is a survival tool, but when abused people grow up, they may experience dissociation habitually and uncontrollably. They may then injure themselves so as to feel something or "feel alive" again. Other people who were abused may use self-injury for the opposite effect—to make overpoweringly painful feelings and memories stop.

People who are abused as children are at risk for NSSI later in life.

People who self-injure often remember terrible childhoods; that may be one reason why they hurt themselves. Victims of abuse are at a high risk for self-injuring if they have no other outlet for their feelings. Abuse does not just have to be physical; it can be emotional as well. For example, Liz C.'s parents were very strict. They did not allow her to go to dances or to movies with friends. Liz was never allowed to display any anger or talk about her feelings. She said her parents were "religious fanatics" who made her believe that any happiness was a sin. Liz began hurting herself in childhood. She hurt herself in many ways, including cutting her arms, scratching and biting herself, and burning her skin with cigarettes. Liz remembered the first time she hurt herself at age 13, after a clash with her mother. She recalled, "You didn't get angry with Mom, because if you did, you would get hurt. I don't know why the idea came across my head—I'm not sure if I was trying to kill myself—but I ended up self-injuring, and I got an immediate release."[18]

Conterio and Lader say that it is easy to understand why abused children grow up to self-injure. They are filled with rage about the way they are treated, but they cannot hurt the people who are cruel to them. Often, they cannot even release the anger in words. Instead of hurting the abuser, they release the rage by hurting themselves. Since such children often grow up believing that they are worthless and deserve to be cruelly treated, many hurt themselves to express self-hate. Often, they feel shame about the abuse and believe that it was their fault. Other self-injurers try to gain control of their bodies through the damage they do. Their bodies were not cared for by people they thought they could trust. Instead, their bodies were treated like objects that could be used. Sometimes, self-injury is a way of reenacting the abuse or trauma. Over and over, by hurting his or her body, the self-injurer relives the previous damage done.

In a strange way, self-injury can even be an emotional way to hurt the abuser. One self-injurer told the therapist who was helping her that she had to cut herself as a way to hurt her mother. She said, "Can't you see? I had to cut her loose!"[19] Researchers say that without strong, loving bonds, abused people cannot feel good about themselves and cannot learn to express their negative feelings in a healthy way. They often cannot even allow themselves to recognize the angry or sad feelings that they experience. Instead, they physically attack themselves, and as time passes they come to depend upon self-injury as a way to survive.

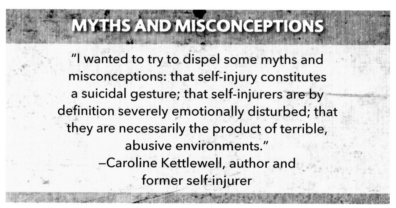

MYTHS AND MISCONCEPTIONS

"I wanted to try to dispel some myths and misconceptions: that self-injury constitutes a suicidal gesture; that self-injurers are by definition severely emotionally disturbed; that they are necessarily the product of terrible, abusive environments."
—Caroline Kettlewell, author and former self-injurer

Quoted in Caroline Kettlewell, *Skin Game* (reading group guide). New York, NY: St. Martin's Press, 1999. images.macmillan.com/folio-assets/readers-guides/9780312263935RG.pdf.

Lack of Warmth, Love, and Acceptance

At least half of all self-injurers, according to clinicians such as Favazza and Conterio, as well as surveys of self-injurers, have never been physically or sexually abused, but psychiatrists Digby Tantam and Nick Huband explain that physical or sexual abuse is not necessary to explain self-injury. People who did not experience warmth and approval from their families may suffer from emotional abuse. They may have grown up feeling neglected or unloved. They may have had strict parents who demanded "perfect" behavior and did not allow their children the freedom to be themselves, express their emotions, or make decisions. The parents may have been cold and controlling or judgmental and critical. They may have treated their children's emotions as trivial, punished them for revealing negative emotions, or denied that their children's feelings were real. This is called invalidating, and some self-injury researchers say that repeated invalidation is a risk factor for self-injury.

Emotional abuse can be as traumatic as physical or sexual abuse.

Tantam and Huband say, "Studies find that there are limited ranges of emotional themes that are likely to trigger self-injury. In our own research, the two that were far and away the most frequent were feeling powerless and feeling uncared for."[20] It is easy to understand that abused children would grow up feeling powerless and uncared for. Even if the self-injurer is not being abused in any way, if they feel out of control of their own life or believe that no one wants to listen to their problems, they may turn to self-harm as a way to deal with those feelings.

Lack of love and acceptance from friends or classmates is also a risk factor for self-harm. A 2013 study published in the *Journal of the American Academy of Child & Adolescent Psychiatry* found that children "who are bullied in elementary school are almost five times more likely to engage in self-harm by the time they are teenagers."[21] The researchers asked nearly 5,000 children in the United Kingdom if they had been bullied between the ages of 7 and 10. After those same children turned 16 or 17, the researchers contacted them again to ask if they had harmed themselves. The study found that 16.5 percent of them had. LGBTQIA teens are particularly at risk because they are often the targets of bullies. Bullying can increase depression, and if victims also have a bad home life or few friends, they may feel as if they have nowhere safe to turn.

The "Safety Catch"

Physical, sexual, and emotional abuse may explain why many people resort to self-injury, but much more research is needed to really understand all of its environmental causes. Since many people are abused and do not become self-injurers, some researchers try to explore human psychology to explain why only some people who have experienced unloving or invalidating environments go on to develop a problem with self-injury. Tantam and Huband suggest that people have a "safety catch,"[22] or neurological response, that protects them from self-injury most of the time. The safety catch is the brain's way of protecting the body. People resist putting themselves in danger of injury and feel disgust and shock when they see or even imagine such injuries because of their safety catch. However, the safety catch can

"They Just Want Attention"

Many people, particularly those who only know about self-harm through books and movies, have ideas about self-injurers that do not reflect reality. One very common and very dangerous idea is that self-injurers only hurt themselves for attention and that this means they should not be given that attention. Some people may say that those who seek attention for their self-harm are not "real" self-injurers, but their injuries are very real. Someone who does show off his or her scars may be desperately seeking attention because he or she feels lonely or depressed and has no idea how to reach out to others in a healthy way. According to the Cornell Research Program on Self-Injury and Recovery:

> For some, self-injury is clearly an attention-seeking act. In this case, it is very important to honor the intent—if someone is injuring him/herself for attention then that person **clearly needs it**—this person is crying out for help. The majority of people who engage in self-injury, however, go to great extremes to hide their cuts, scars, or burns. Although not overtly attention-seeking, hidden self-injury is still a symptom of underlying distress and it merits attention from others who are in a position to help.[1]

1. Saskya Caicedo and Janis Whitlock, "Top 15 Misconceptions of Self-Injury," The Cornell Research Program on Self-Injury and Recovery, 2009. www.selfinjury.bctr.cornell.edu/documents/15_misconceptions.pdf.

be turned off or weakened if the type of self-injury is familiar or culturally acceptable. For example, in Germany during the 19th century, a scar on the face from a sword injury was honorable, so young men would cut each other or themselves with sabres to have a fashionable scar. The safety catch that protects people from harm is weakened in these situations. For most people, however, the idea of slashing an arm with a razor blade on purpose is socially unacceptable, shocking, and repulsive because of their safety catch.

Tantam and Huband say that self-injurers are able to overcome or bypass their safety catch even though their actions are not familiar or accepted by society. Repeating self-injury actions is one way to overcome the safety catch. The individual gets more and more used to the sight and feeling of the injury and no longer is repulsed or shocked by the experience. Another way to overcome the safety catch is through social familiarity and cultural acceptance, such as the bloodletting that is done in some tribes in New Guinea to initiate boys into manhood or the self-whipping that used to be practiced by some Christian groups in Europe. Psychiatrists and psychologists have also reported extreme self-injury in some severely mentally ill people and in children born with certain serious brain disorders, and in these cases, they suggest that the normal safety catch may be neurologically disrupted or turned off.

Vulnerability in Our Genetics

Some researchers wonder whether the vulnerability to self-injury lies in the genes. Genes are the units of heredity in all living things. Most genes in humans are the same for everyone, but variations and changes in certain genes can determine whether a person is at risk for developing some problems or illnesses or is vulnerable to certain experiences in the environment. Scientists think that a variation in a gene or genes could possibly predispose some individuals to developing a self-injury disorder when the environment "pulls the trigger." A trigger for self-harm, for example, might be sexual abuse during childhood. An individual with certain gene variations might become a self-injurer when exposed to sexual abuse.

So far, the theory that a genetic vulnerability causes some to self-harm has yet to be proven as fact, but a recent study suggests that researchers may be on the right track. In 2010, veterinary researchers reported discovering a gene in Doberman pinscher dogs that was linked with compulsive behavior. The dogs with the gene variation exhibited compulsive behavior, such as licking themselves until they caused open wounds on their bodies. The veterinarians reported that the dogs developed this behavior in response to anxiety or stress. Nicholas Dodman, the leader of the research team, said that people with OCD who injure themselves may have a similar gene variation. Other researchers now are trying to find out whether this is true. If it is, the gene or genes would not exactly cause the kind of self-injury sometimes seen with OCD. However, the genetic variation might explain why some people, when exposed to negative environmental triggers, would develop self-harm behaviors.

Research on animals who harm themselves, such as Doberman pinschers, may help scientists better understand self-injury in humans.

Another study in 2012 studied twins and self-harm rates to differentiate the roles of genetics and environment in self-harm behaviors. The results showed that there were hereditary impacts on self-injury rates, which shows that genetics may play a larger role than people think. Thoughts of self-harm and suicide are suggested by these results to stem from a combination of genetic and environmental risk factors.

Harvard psychologist Matthew K. Nock also believes that gene variations could make people vulnerable to psychological disorders if they are exposed to environmental triggers and stress. He suggests that gene variations may make people more impulsive, more emotionally reactive, and less able to cope with stress. In an abusive or negative environment, such people may become anxious, depressed, and self-destructive. They may develop drug abuse problems, eating disorders, suicidal thoughts, and self-injury disorders. Many people who self-injure also have eating disorders, substance abuse problems, and psychological disorders such as depression and anxiety. Many also attempt or think about suicide. Nock suggests that all of these problems are just different forms of self-destructive behaviors, caused by the interaction between genes and life experiences. However, he warns that the true causes of self-injury are complex and that scientists are just beginning to understand how gene vulnerabilities and environmental triggers interact to cause psychological disorders. He explains that the idea of "'a gene for' behaviors such as self-injury is unrealistic and inaccurate."[23]

Addictive Qualities of Self-Injury

When the safety catch is overcome, repeated acts of self-injury become easier, and people may develop a kind of addiction to the behavior. Many people who self-injure report feeling little or no pain while they are hurting themselves, even when their wounds are deep or serious. This happens because the brain releases chemicals called endorphins whenever it receives pain signals from an injury. Tracy Alderman explained that endorphins act almost like morphine to reduce the amount of pain people feel. They are the body's way of reducing the stress that pain causes. She said, "Sometimes, people who intentionally hurt themselves will even say that they felt a 'rush' or 'high' from the act. Given the role of endorphins, this makes perfect sense."[24]

Psychologist V. J. Turner argued that self-injury becomes habit-forming and addictive in the same way that some drugs become addictive. She said that the chemicals released by the brain in response to self-injury can "hook" people just as drugs such as heroin and cocaine do. She explained that being vulnerable to addiction may be rooted in traumatic childhood experiences, psychological or personality disorders, or being born with a vulnerability, or predisposition, to becoming addicted to substances or behaviors.

Many people who self-injure agree with Turner that self-injury is addictive, which is why they continue to do it even when they experience feelings of shame or guilt afterward. Justin Mills, who struggled with his self-injury addiction in the past, remembered cutting his legs with a razor blade every day for three years. When he was not cutting, he described himself as

For many, self-harm can be just as addictive as drugs or alcohol.

Self-Injury in the Animal Kingdom

Studying animal behavior can give scientists an idea of what to look for in humans. Experimental psychologists have reported self-injurious behavior in many animals, such as monkeys, lions, hyenas, rats, birds, dogs, and cats. The animals may lick themselves until sores develop, bite themselves, or tear at the skin with their claws. Researchers say that social isolation is a major reason for the behavior in captive animals. In small zoo or laboratory cages, animals are "prisoners," often isolated and separated from others of their kind.

Frustration is another cause of animal self-injury. For example, a captive animal may redirect its aggression from the human it cannot attack to its own body. It may be frustrated by an inability to reach food that it can see and, therefore, direct its aggression toward its body. A captive or domestic animal may be so frustrated by boredom or lack of stimulation that it compulsively licks or scratches itself or pulls out feathers or fur.

Some psychologists say that animal self-injury is very similar to self-injury in people. It is the result of anxiety in stressful situations in which the animal is powerless and has no control. The animals' self-injury becomes a way of coping—a way to reduce extreme stress.

Some animals in captivity exhibit self-harm behaviors due to feelings of frustration and powerlessness.

feeling angry, depressed, helpless, and desperate. Cutting was like a drug for him that let him escape his terrible emotions. He says now he knows that "one must be in a certain hopeless state of mind in order to feel the effects of the drug."[25]

A Blank Slate: Self-Injury as a Learned Behavior

While some researchers suggest that self-injury can have genetic causes, Turner argues that it is learned. First the self-injurer must experiment with harming himself or herself. Then, as he or she learns about the feeling of release or the soothing "benefits" or the "high," the action slowly becomes addictive. The urge to self-injure grows stronger and becomes more difficult to resist, even when the individual wants to stop. Self-injury becomes the drug that numbs emotional pain. As time passes, the self-injurer requires deeper and deeper damage to get the medicating effects, just like drug addicts need more and more drugs to get high.

Indeed, Mills first got the idea of cutting himself from a girlfriend. She self-injured by cutting her legs. One day, when he was feeling extremely angry and did not know how to get rid of the feeling, he impulsively tried cutting his own leg. Gradually, the cutting habit became more severe and more frequent.

Many self-injury experts believe that the habit of injuring oneself may begin by imitation or example. Mills imitated his girlfriend, and some researchers have reported that other self-injurers first learned of the behavior from friends at school. In one 2010 study of middle and high schoolers, researchers Janis Whitlock and Amanda Purington of Cornell University found groups of teens self-injuring together as a kind of sign of group membership.

Some researchers wonder whether self-injury might be contagious. In prisons, psychiatric treatment hospitals, and other residential settings, self-injury behaviors seem to spread among the populations like a sickness. In middle and high schools, teachers and counselors have reported epidemics of self-injury that seem to spread among students. However, in 1989, Favazza and Conterio reported that 91 percent of 240 female self-injurers in a research study had not known anyone who self-injured nor even heard of the behavior before they experimented with it or accidentally discovered it. Whitlock surveyed 2,875 college students in 2006 and discovered that more than one-third of those who self-injured had kept the behavior a secret from everyone. Studies such as these suggest that imitation of others is often not a factor in self-harm. Nevertheless, on the basis of other studies in 2006 and 2009, the Cornell research team that includes Whitlock, Purington, and others says about some self-injurers, "Our research suggests that the Internet and the increasing prevalence of self-injury in popular media, such as movies, books, and news reports … may play a role in the spread of self-injury."[26]

Whitlock explained that self-injury may be spread through a school or any social group because learning about instances of self-injury makes it seem socially acceptable and helps to weaken the safety catch against self-injury for other individuals. In a residential group, such as a prison or hospital, it is relatively easy to hear about or see the evidence of self-injury. In the larger society, modern use of the Internet can also make it simple to learn about instances of self-injury.

Whitlock says that in the anonymity of the Internet, young people can connect with others who self-injure and come to think of the behavior as normal and acceptable. They may be encouraged and supported in experimenting with self-injury. However, Whitlock believes the encouragement to self-injure increases or starts the behavior only in vulnerable people. A happy, well-adjusted teen, for example, would not become addicted to self-injury simply by discovering a website where people discuss harming themselves. Contagion—or "catching" the behavior through contact and discussions with other self-injurers—would occur only among teens who do not know how to cope with their negative emotions and have "a low sense of self-worth."[27]

The Research Continues

Research into the biological, environmental, and psychological causes of self-injury is just beginning, and scientists do not fully

Katy Perry wrote a song called "Self Inflicted" that compares heartbreak to NSSI. Some experts fear that descriptions of self-injury in songs, movies, and books may encourage others to try it.

understand all the causes. Nock calls self-injury both "perplexing" and "harmful" and says that many important questions remain unanswered. He says of the research so far:

> Although impressive gains have been made, there is still much to learn about why people intentionally and repeatedly harm themselves. Future research on self-injury will not only advance the understanding, assessment, and treatment of this behavior problem, but will also improve the understanding of self-harm more broadly and of how to decrease such behaviors in order to help people live healthier and more adaptive lives.[28]

CHAPTER 3

Inherent Risks of Self-Injury

Therapy is a key component of treatment for self-harm and the underlying issues that cause it, but it can be difficult for a self-injurer to get the treatment he or she needs. One reason is the secretive nature of NSSI; sufferers will often attempt to hide their scars under clothing or claim that they are normal injuries, such as scratches from a cat or bruises from accidentally running into furniture. Another reason is that they may trick themselves into thinking that their self-injury is not a risky or negative action but a positive one—self-preserving and no different than any other coping tool. Karen Conterio and Wendy Lader say that arguments for this view include:

"Self-injury doesn't hurt anyone."
"Giving up self-injury will only make me hurt more."
"If I don't self-injure, I'll end up killing myself."
"It's my body and I can do whatever I want."
"No one knows that I injure anyway."
"I don't understand why it upsets others."[29]

Most professionals and experts see self-injury as self-destructive. As time goes on, most self-injurers come to agree. Self-injury is not a positive way to deal with life. The risks of the behavior are physical, emotional, and social, and repetitive self-injurers do not learn healthy ways to cope with stress and pain.

The Lethality of Self-Injury

Self-injury researcher Barent W. Walsh says that most self-injury carries little risk of permanent disability or death. He calls this common type of self-injury "low-lethality." However, a nontypical kind of self-injury, called major self-injury, can result in real

Exercise helps reduce stress, anxiety, and depression. It is a healthy alternative to self-harm.

medical danger. It is called "medium-lethality" or "high-lethality,"[30] depending on the severity of the injury. Major self-injury includes any injury that causes major damage to the body, such as deliberately breaking bones. In the Western world, acts of major self-injury are generally committed by people who have a mental illness that impairs their ability to fully understand the consequences of their self-harming actions. This kind of self-injury can lead to permanent harm and death.

In other parts of the world, major self-injury may not be a result of mental illness but an extreme cry for help or an expression of hopeless, helpless despair. In Afghanistan, for example, major self-injury is common among women. Afghan women have few rights and are often badly mistreated. They may be beaten and abused by their husbands or in-laws, are often forced into arranged marriages at young ages, and receive little support or help from the government or society. They may also suffer from disorders associated with self-harm, such as anxiety and depression, but may not have access to mental health care. Sometimes, these desperate women resort to pouring fuel on their bodies and setting themselves on fire. This practice is also referred to as self-immolation. In many of these cases, the women are choosing suicide to escape terrible situations, but at other times, the women are self-injuring in a very dangerous way in order to demonstrate their misery and stop their ongoing physical and emotional pain. The exact number of women who do this is impossible to find; attempted suicide is considered a sin, so many people feel embarrassed when a woman in their family attempts self-immolation and deny that it happened. Additionally, if a woman lives in an area without good medical care, there is no hospital record to show that she hurt herself.

In 2008, filmmaker Olga Sadat went to Afghanistan to interview women in hospitals who had set themselves on fire. As she gained their trust, several of the women told Sadat about the circumstances that led to their self-injuries. Sadat reported that their aim was not suicide. The women hoped that they would be rescued. They wanted the people who were abusing them to understand how much they were suffering. They hoped these family members would stop them and show that they were valued. Often, the family members did nothing until it was too late. Sadly, this kind of major self-injury is often fatal in a country where advanced medical treatment for severe burns is not available. Of the women Sadat interviewed, only one recovered from her injuries; the rest died. Across the country, 70 percent of women who set fire to themselves die of their injuries.

Medical Risks with Common Self-Injury

Common self-injury in the industrialized world rarely carries the risk of death, but it does carry other medical risks, especially when self-injury is repetitive and impulsive. Self-injurers may pick at the cuts, not allowing them to heal, which can lead to infection. A British magazine for nurses, *Nursing Times*, warned:

> *People who injure themselves risk infections if their wounds are not treated properly. Cuts can become infected if a person uses non-sterile or dirty cutting instruments. It is also important not to share cutting implements with other people as many diseases, including HIV and AIDS, can be caught this way. They are also at risk of permanent scarring from the cuts and wounds.*[31]

Wounds from cutting can also be so deep or bleed so much that medical treatment is necessary. According to experts, about 1 in 5 self-injurers accidentally makes a life-threatening injury. If they try to keep the injury secret, as many of them do, they may not get the immediate medical care they need in these situations.

Sometimes, self-harm can lead to a real medical emergency.

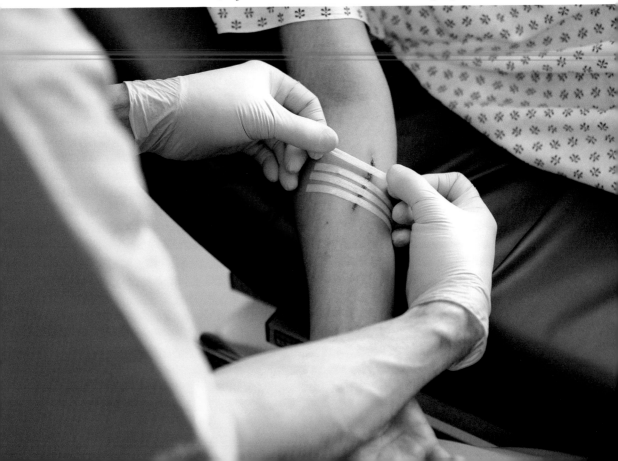

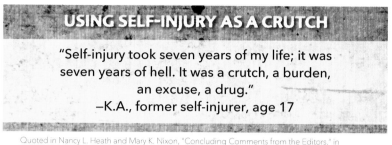

USING SELF-INJURY AS A CRUTCH

"Self-injury took seven years of my life; it was seven years of hell. It was a crutch, a burden, an excuse, a drug."
–K.A., former self-injurer, age 17

Quoted in Nancy L. Heath and Mary K. Nixon, "Concluding Comments from the Editors," in *Self-Injury in Youth: The Essential Guide to Assessment and Intervention.* New York: Routledge, 2009, p. 317.

Just as when drug users develop a tolerance to a drug and must use more of it to get the same result, people who are addicted to self-injury often make deeper and deeper cuts as time goes on. Then the risks of medical complications become very real. A self-injurer named Jennifer wrote an online article about her experience making too deep of a cut. She tried to treat the injury herself and even went to school the next day, but after about 20 hours, she was getting weak and dizzy. She realized that she could not really stop the bleeding completely nor keep the wound closed. As eventually happens with many self-injurers in her situation, she had to go to the nearest emergency room. There, her wound was cleaned and finally closed with 31 stitches. Her experience convinced Jennifer that her self-cutting had to stop. She wrote, "This can't keep happening. It just can't. That's all."[32] When people say that their self-injury does not hurt anyone, Conterio and Lader ask, "What about you, the self-injurer? You are important, and you are clearly getting hurt—emotionally as well as physically."[33]

Temporary Relief from Long-Lasting Pain

The risks of self-injury are indeed emotional as well as physical. When people say that they have to use self-injury as a survival tool, either to avoid suicide or to stop their emotional pain, experts point out that the coping tool does not really work. The emotional relief from self-injury does not last. The intense emotions return, and the self-injurer never learns how to cope with strong emotions or relieve tension and stress in healthy ways. That is why professionals consider self-injury to be a poor

Self-Embedding

In 2008, doctors at the Nationwide Children's Hospital in Chicago reported that about 10 to 20 percent of teens who self-injure insert foreign objects under their skin. This is called self-embedding. William Shiels, one of the hospital doctors, said serious infections can result. He explained, "The infections aren't just at the site. You can get a deep muscle infection or a bone infection."[1] If the embedded objects are not removed, they may also travel to other sites in the body, such as organs, and cause tears or other damage.

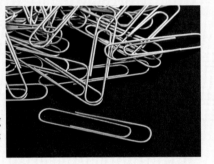

Self-embedding means inserting objects under the skin, such as paper clips or staples.

1. Quoted in Tiffany Sharples, "Teens' Latest Self-Injury Fad: Self-Embedding," *TIME*, December 11, 2008. content.time.com/time/health/article/0,8599,1865995,00.html.

coping tool and self-destructive in the long run. One online self-injury forum explained:

> One of the problems with self-injury as a coping mechanism is that its effects are only temporary. Once the endorphins dissipate [fade away] and the consequences of hurting yourself become clear, you may experience feelings of guilt, shame, and remorse. Also, the negative feelings you experienced before hurting yourself may come back at this point or shortly thereafter. So, as a result of self-injury, you may feel even worse than you did before hurting yourself. And these negative emotions can be the beginnings of another act of self-injury.[34]

Self-injury has been called a temporary solution to a permanent problem. When it is used to block out negative emotions, it can seem like a "quick fix," but this solution stops people from dealing with their underlying pain. That is why Deb Martinson calls self-injury a "crude and ultimately self-destructive tool."[35] People do not heal the underlying emotional problems when they depend on self-injury. They do not rid themselves of the feelings of self-hate, shame, depression, helplessness, fear, tension, or any of the traumas or past experiences that they are trying to numb. They do not learn healthy coping tools.

Destructive Aftermath

Often, self-injury episodes increase the negative feelings that people have about themselves, the Mayo Clinic said. The aftermath of a self-injury episode can be an increase in feelings of shame, guilt, and low self-esteem. This happens because self-injurers feel embarrassed and ashamed about the behavior. They may fear being "crazy" or "sick." They may hate themselves for

Self-harm can create a cycle of loneliness: Some people hurt themselves because they feel lonely, but their fear of letting anyone know their secret keeps them from getting close to anyone.

losing control if they have been trying to resist self-injuring. They may feel sure that other people would judge them with disgust, horror, and shock. They may be disgusted with themselves for causing wounds and feel ugly because of the permanent scars. They often feel isolated and alone, unworthy of reassurance and support from friends or loved ones. Because of these feelings, many self-injurers become secretive with and withdrawn from the very people that they wish to be close to, love, and trust.

Impacts on Relationships

Self-hate, loneliness, and loss of social connections are three of the biggest emotional risks of self-injury. Drawing information from Tracy Alderman's book *The Scarred Soul*, one self-injury help website explained that

> self-injury encourages emotional distance from other people in several ways. First, "the secrecy and shame attached to many SI [self-injury] behaviors causes a lack of honesty and open communication between you and the important other in your life." You may have not told anyone about your self-injury. You may edit information about your self-injury and about how you feel (your emotional states.) You may even lie about what you do and how you feel. Each of these hinders or cuts off communication and intimacy with other people, which creates distance. You can't be close with others if you are lying to them.[36]

On another website for people with self-injury problems, several individuals described their feelings of self-hate and the ways they felt cut off from other people. A girl identifying herself as Charlotte wrote about her cutting, "I felt I had to punish myself, but now when I look at my scars and look back on what I did I feel so ashamed and angry with myself. I really hate myself sometimes, my cutting has left me a lot of scars … on my arms legs and stomach and I wish they were not there."[37] Other people on the site described themselves as cowardly, weak, friendless, scared, or freakish for hurting themselves. Like many self-injurers, they said they wished for sympathy and understanding. However, their desire to keep their habit a secret and their invented belief that they were bad people for harming themselves made it difficult for them to tell anyone who would be sympathetic to them.

Seeking Medical Help

Doctors, nurses, and other medical personnel may have as difficult a time coping with self-injury as do family and friends. Those who have not been properly trained or have never seen such injuries before may react negatively. Self-injury experts explain that negative reactions are something self-injurers may unfortunately face because of a lack of awareness, even in the medical profession, about self-injury. Experts such as Deb Martinson and the researchers at Cornell University are involved in outreach efforts to medical personnel to educate them about self-injury. However, most doctors and nurses are used to seeing injuries much worse than those self-injurers give themselves and have received training in how to act professionally when they see wounds.

Seeking Help

Self-injury is almost always done in private, but eventually, most people who self-injure are either discovered or make the decision to tell someone else about the problem. Family or friends may see the wounds or scars. Medical treatment may be needed, leading hospital personnel to question the nature of the injury. The self-injurer may find the burden of secrecy to be too great and confide in someone or ask for help. It is a risky, frightening time, both for the self-injurer and for the person who is learning about the problem. The person who self-injures is risking negative reactions. These reactions may isolate the self-injurer still further. Even when the reactions are supportive and loving, however, self-injury can cause pain and fear in other people.

When people are overwhelmed and afraid, they sometimes react very badly. Conterio and Lader explained, "Self-preservation is a basic instinct. Abandoning that instinct seems frightening, crazy, or at the very least counterintuitive to people who don't self-injure."[38] Many people are not taught enough about self-harm to be able to understand it right away. This can make a self-injurer feel angry and hurt, and possibly stop him or her from opening up to anyone else.

To lower the risk of someone reacting badly, timing is one important factor. Nigel Sampson, a specialist in adolescent mental health, said:

> It has to be the right time for you and the other person ... Only tell them when you're 100 [percent] sure it's the right time for you. Wait until the other person is calm. Be honest and say you have something to share and that it may be a shock, but that you're looking for help, not sympathy.[39]

Another important thing to consider is who to tell. It should be a trusted friend or adult who will not make the self-injurer feel bad or tell other people their secret. Sampson advised:

> Whoever it is, set boundaries around the conversation ... Just because you are telling that person, it doesn't give them permission to tell everyone else. Make sure the person you're about to tell is someone you can rely on. Pick someone you know well who won't get angry. Be clear that you're telling them to seek help and that this doesn't mean you'll stop self-harming just because you've told someone.[40]

A supportive friend will be able to help a self-injurer take steps toward recovery.

Although the act of telling a trusted person is a good first step, it is not a cure for self-harm. The self-injurer still needs treatment from a psychiatric professional. However, most people will ask or demand that the self-injurer stop because they are afraid for the person's safety. It is important for the self-injurer to be able to explain that it is not a behavior that can be stopped overnight. They should also be prepared to tell their confidante exactly what they need, whether it is someone to sit with them at the hospital, help seeking a therapist, or simply someone to talk to.

The conversation about self-harm is likely to be uncomfortable and painful even if the self-injurer has chosen an understanding person. A friend or family member who loves the self-injurer may react poorly out of fear for the self-injurer's safety, especially if they are given too much information at one time. Sampson suggests continuing the conversation at a later time if it starts to become too emotional.

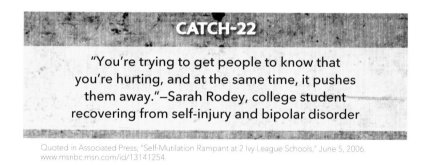

CATCH-22

"You're trying to get people to know that you're hurting, and at the same time, it pushes them away."—Sarah Rodey, college student recovering from self-injury and bipolar disorder

Quoted in Associated Press; "Self-Mutilation Rampant at 2 Ivy League Schools," June 5, 2006. www.msnbc.msn.com/id/13141254.

Impact on Others

Of course, most parents, family, and friends do want to help, and they are upset and hurt when they learn the secret. Alderman explained that initial reactions to self-injury include "shock and denial," "anger and frustration," "empathy, sympathy, and sadness," and "guilt."[41] The shock and denial happen because it is so hard for others to understand bypassing the safety catch and damaging oneself on purpose. As a result, people who learn about self-injury want to make the self-injurer stop and feel helpless and horrified when they cannot. They may also feel angry that the self-injurer was deceiving them about the wounds and scars (for example, excusing wounds by saying they are due to cat scratches or falls or accidents). Family and friends may also feel that the behavior is somehow their fault. They worry that they did something to cause their loved one to self-injure, and they think that they have failed—as a parent, best friend, or even a good teacher. They may also feel guilty for not noticing earlier that something was wrong.

People who care about a person who self-injures often feel fear. They are afraid of permanent injury or that the injury will escalate to suicide. They want desperately to make the self-injury stop. For a parent, sometimes this means trying to control the environment of a self-injurer. Parents may think that they should hide all the sharp implements in the house or watch over their child constantly so that he or she cannot self-injure. However, fear is not good for relationships. Trust is lost, and the person who self-injures feels defensive, misunderstood, and belittled. Rather than try to control the situation themselves, parents should let a trained medical professional work with the self-injurer. The role of parents and friends is to give emotional support, not to try to "fix" the sufferer.

Escape the Cycle

Self-injurers would stop hurting themselves if only they knew how. They are scared and hurting, too. Wanting to stop and learning to do so are the only ways to reduce the risks of self-injury, but the hurting cannot stop until the self-injurer makes the decision to stop. Even then, establishing good relationships, giving up self-injury, and recovering can be a long and difficult road, especially when self-injury feels like the only way to cope and survive. However, people who have been through that journey report that ending their cycle of self-harm was one of the best decisions of their lives.

The Recovery Process

As research continues and experts attempt to nail down the root causes of self-injury, the recovery process can be a bit of a struggle. Therapy is a good way to treat NSSI and the disorders it is associated with, but there is no single best treatment for everyone. Even experts argue about which should be treated first, the self-harming behaviors or the underlying mental conditions. In fact, every sufferer brings to the table a unique set of variables in personality, situations, problems, disorders, and needs that can change the situation. Fortunately, experts and recovering self-injurers agree that healing is possible. No one need resign themselves to a life of self-injurious suffering. When the decision is made to try, then healing is an option.

Therapy can seem overwhelming at first, but it is an important part of recovery.

Recovery today focuses on respect for oneself, as well as emphasizing the need for healthy coping skills, nonjudgmental exploration of emotional needs, and compassion for the overwhelming feelings that can lead to self-harm. The approach to these treatments may involve hospitalization or residential treatment programs in more serious cases. Those who fall somewhere in the middle may opt for outpatient therapy. The Internet can also be helpful; self-injurers can find support and empathy from fellow sufferers or recovering self-injurers on self-injury websites, although these should not be used as a replacement for therapy.

Karen Conterio and Wendy Lader, who run one kind of treatment program, offer this encouragement: "Everyone who has ever self-injured and stopped is eager to pass the message along about how this soul-destroying behavior can be overcome. Our patients' message is that the road to recovery is bumpy indeed, but is the best journey they ever took."[42]

Beginning the Recovery Process

Tracy Alderman says to people who self-injure, "First, you need to want to stop. Without that, you won't be successful."[43] Recognizing that self-injury is a destructive tool and wanting to escape the cycle of repetitive self-injury is absolutely necessary for any treatment or therapy to work. Nobody can be forced to stop self-injuring against their will.

Conterio and Lader, who established treatment programs called S.A.F.E. (Self-Abuse Finally Ends) Alternatives, agree with Alderman. They say that treatment must be voluntary and that the self-injurer must be committed to change. This does not necessarily mean that the individual is sure he or she can change; he or she may be terrified, unsure how to survive without self-injury, and overwhelmed by the idea of giving up self-injury. However, the self-injurer needs to have come to a point of really wanting to stop.

Jennifer wanted to stop self-injury because the deep wounds she had accidentally inflicted scared her. Justin Mills reached a point at which he felt hopelessness, and "it was ingrained in my mind that cutting would progressively destroy my life."[44] Liz C.

wanted to quit self-injuring when she realized that it did not calm and soothe her the way it used to do. Some self-injurers stop when they can no longer tolerate the feelings of hopelessness, guilt, and shame many experience after self-injuring. Others may be motivated by the pain and distress of loved ones and friends who insist that the self-injurer get help. Some decide to take the first step toward recovery when they find themselves missing work or school and unable to function in society because they self-injure so frequently. Many seek treatment when they find themselves frightened because self-injury no longer brings relief from intense negative emotions, and this situation triggers or increases suicidal thoughts.

Residential Treatment Options

Whatever the reasons for wanting to stop self-injuring, few people are able to do so without professional help, and residential programs are one way of getting that help. There are residential treatment centers across the country that specialize in helping people who suffer from a variety of mental disorders and destructive behaviors, including self-injury. Treatment plans vary from center to center and person to person, but may include therapy strategies such as group therapy, individual therapy, music and art therapy, cognitive behavioral therapy (CBT), and dialectical behavior therapy (DBT).

The length of stay at a residential center may also vary depending on how severe the person's self-harming behaviors are and how quickly he or she progresses through therapy. At residential centers, staff members do not try to control the patients; instead, they try to help self-injurers take responsibility for their own safety and stop feeling powerless and helpless. Although a residential stay can be helpful for some people, it may be harmful for others. Experts have found that when teens with emotional problems live together in large groups, they can transfer their behaviors to each other. In other words, someone who is in treatment only for an eating disorder may start to self-injure because some of his or her fellow patients do. This is known as a contagion effect. Fortunately, because experts understand that this is a problem, they can take precautions to prevent the spread of risky behaviors in residential settings.

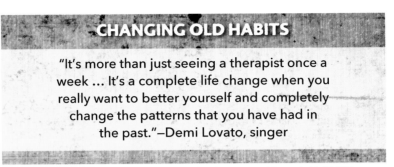

CHANGING OLD HABITS

"It's more than just seeing a therapist once a week ... It's a complete life change when you really want to better yourself and completely change the patterns that you have had in the past."—Demi Lovato, singer

Quoted in Amy Sciarretto, "Demi Lovato Sheds Light in *SELF* Interview," Popcrush, July 17, 2012. popcrush.com/demi-lovato-light-self-interview-photos/.

Finding a Therapist

Self-injurers who are not an immediate danger to themselves will often seek outpatient therapy instead of residential therapy. This means the patient continues to live at home and go to school or work as normal, but also sees a therapist, typically for one hour every week, although the frequency of appointments can vary depending on how quickly the patient needs to resolve his or her injurious behavior.

Finding a therapist can be a tricky process. There is no one right method or person for everyone. A person who self-injures may start going to one therapist and find that he or she does not like or trust that person. It is perfectly acceptable for someone to choose a different therapist whose personality and approach to the problem fits with the patient's wants and needs. For example, some patients may want to joke around about their problems, while others want to speak about them seriously. Finding a therapist who can match the patient's tone is very important in this case. It is up to the patient to do research, ask questions, and trust their instincts when it comes to finding a therapist. Finding the right person may be a stressful and time-consuming task, but therapy is no use if the patient is not comfortable with the person he or she is working with, so it is well worth the effort. Asking a friend or trusted adult to help may make the process easier.

Some red flags, or bad signs, to consider when searching for a therapist to help with self-injury issues include:

- They do not discuss the patients' rights in the first session and do not have the patient sign a confidentiality agreement.
- They do not have experience helping people with NSSI.
- They recommend things that go against what the patient believes in.
- They do not answer any questions, or give confusing or conflicting answers.
- They share too much information about their own lives.
- The patient does not feel progress is being made after several sessions.
- They roll their eyes, make rude comments, say things sarcastically, or do other things to make the patient feel judged or shamed.
- They do not remember basic things about the patient (for example, getting the patient's name wrong).
- They answer phone calls, e-mails, or texts during the session.
- The patient feels so uncomfortable with the therapist (not with the process of sharing his or her feelings) that he or she starts thinking about skipping sessions.

Patients should feel comfortable enough with their therapist to speak up when something is not working. It is important to remember that patients are allowed to switch therapists at any time if they feel their current therapist is not the right fit for them.

DBT: A Popular Therapy Approach

Therapists have a variety of styles to choose from when treating a patient. Some specialize in one particular style; others may use a combination based on what they feel is best for a particular patient. CBT is an approach that is commonly used to treat several of the underlying issues associated with NSSI, including anxiety, depression, and PTSD. It focuses on identifying negative thoughts and changing them to positive ones, which can change the way a person feels. Through techniques such as journaling and relaxation, patients "learn new coping skills in order to better handle their issues, develop more positive beliefs and behaviors, and may even resolve long-standing life problems."[45]

DBT is a form of CBT that several studies have found to be particularly effective for people who suffer from BPD and NSSI. *Counseling Today* says that "DBT, which combines individual therapy, group skills training, and family education, has emerged as one of the most effective treatments for adolescents who are suicidal and/or self-injure."[46] It is not a perfect solution for everyone, but it can be combined with other types of therapy to create a method that will work for the individual. This type of therapy

> helps a person identify their strengths and builds on them so that the person can feel better about him/herself and their life ... helps identify thoughts, beliefs, and assumptions that make life harder ... [and] requires constant attention to relationships between clients and staff ... DBT asks people to complete homework assignments, to role-play new ways of interacting with others, and to practice skills such as soothing yourself when upset ... The individual therapist helps the person to learn, apply, and master the DBT skills.[47]

Group sessions are a key part of DBT.

People undergoing DBT typically have weekly one-on-one sessions as well as weekly group sessions. The group sessions teach participants how to manage their emotions, set healthy boundaries with other people, practice mindfulness (concentrating on the present instead of their fears about the future), and deal with stress in non-injurious ways.

Alternatives to Self-Injury

Some therapists may have patients make a list of comforting, soothing, or distracting activities that are alternatives to self-injury. Some possible alternatives include keeping a journal or writing in an impulse-control log, listening to music, talking to a friend or counselor, taking a walk, or working on a hobby or craft project. Even though it is very painful to do, one important alternative is to sit quietly and experience one's feelings. This alternative helps people realize that the feelings will not drive them crazy or kill them, that they can feel uncomfortable without harming themselves, and that they can accept and tolerate negative emotions.

Writing as Therapy

A key part of CBT and DBT therapy is the use of a journal to help patients make sense of their emotions. The idea is to focus on exploring feelings, communicating thoughts, and making sense of why self-injury became a problem in the first place.

All of the tools in the therapy toolbox help people to stop and think when they get the desire to self-injure. Over time, they help people become empowered to resist their urges. As they succeed,

Many find that keeping a journal is an effective coping mechanism to help avoid self-harm habits.

they become confident that they can lead an injury-free life. While they use the tools, people explore underlying feelings with their therapists and learn new coping strategies for their feelings of isolation, self-hate, shame, and powerlessness. They learn that they are not helpless and worthless at all. They learn to take responsibility for their own safety and to heal.

Sample No-Harm Contract

Every patient in a S.A.F.E. Alternatives treatment program signs a contract as one requirement of admission. This is one example of the kind of contract that might be used:

As a candidate for the S.A.F.E. Alternatives program, I recognize that self-injury interferes with all aspects of my life. I am committed to treatment of my problem and to stopping all self-injurious behavior. I am aware of and agree to the following guidelines for my treatment:

1. *No self-damaging or property-damaging behavior throughout my hospital stay.*

2. *If I have a concurrent eating disorder, I agree to follow treatment recommendations to address this problem.*

3. *Sexual contact with others, physical threats, assaultive behavior, stealing, use of nonprescribed drugs, or use of alcohol may lead to dismissal from the S.A.F.E. Alternatives program.*

4. *Elopement [running away] will automatically lead to discharge.*[1]

1. Karen Conterio and Wendy Lader, *Bodily Harm*. New York, NY: Hyperion, 1998, p. 297.

Controversy Surrounding Contracts

Some therapy programs, such as Conterio and Lader's S.A.F.E. Alternatives program, start with the patient signing a no-harm or no-suicide contract. This contract states that the person undergoing therapy agrees not to self-harm or attempt suicide during the course of treatment. Some therapists believe the reminder of the contract gives recovering self-injurers an incentive not to relapse. However, the use of self-harm contracts is controversial. Studies have shown that no-harm contracts are of little value for people who are suicidal, and their value for people who self-injure is not accepted by everyone. Barent Walsh, for example, is an expert therapist who treats people who self-injure. He says, "I generally recommend against using Safety Contracts as a strategy to deal with self-injury, because they often have more risks than benefits."[48] Dr. Stacey Freedenthal, a psychotherapist and researcher, agrees that if such contracts worked, the patients would not actually need therapy; instead, they could simply "call on their strengths, resources, and self-control to manage their impulses and stay safe on their own. The task of therapy is to build those assets, not to presume that they exist."[49] Instead of a safety contract, Freedenthal recommends the use of safety planning, where the patient and therapist work together to find ways to keep a self-injurer or suicidal person safe.

Walsh believes that such contracts just encourage people to keep their self-injury episodes a secret from their therapists. It is much too difficult, he says, to tolerate the emotional distress or feelings of emptiness without self-injury. Clients who self-injure after promising the therapist not to may feel like failures, feel misunderstood, and drop out of therapy. Their symptoms of psychological disorder may even get worse.

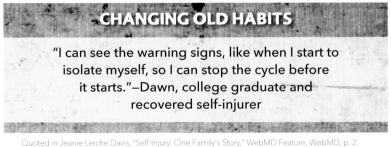

CHANGING OLD HABITS

"I can see the warning signs, like when I start to isolate myself, so I can stop the cycle before it starts."–Dawn, college graduate and recovered self-injurer

Quoted in Jeanie Lerche Davis, "Self-Injury: One Family's Story," WebMD Feature, WebMD, p. 2. www.webmd.com/anxiety-panic/features/self-injury-one-familys-story.

He explains that people cannot give up the coping tool of self-injury until they have learned other, healthy coping tools that can replace the self-injury. Learning new coping tools can take a long time in therapy. Walsh urges other professionals, "Do not ask self-injurers to give up the behavior before they are ready."[50] Many other therapists and clinicians agree with Walsh because in their own treatment experiences, they have discovered that restriction of self-injury behaviors has worsened emotional health or even led to suicide attempts in their patients.

Transition to Replacement Skills

Unless a client asks for a contract or is in serious danger from severe self-injury, Walsh believes in therapy that concentrates on resolving underlying emotional problems and teaching replacement skills instead of immediately preventing the self-injury. The idea is to make a gradual transition from self-injury behaviors to more healthy choices.

No one treatment method is known to work best for self-injury, so Walsh says that several different treatment methods may be useful for developing the ability to stop self-injury. Through talking with the therapist, the self-injurer may explore his or her thoughts and beliefs—such as whether he or she is "bad," should feel shame, deserves punishment, is powerless and helpless, or is unlovable and worthless.

Other talk therapies might concentrate on the self-injurer's body image. People who have been sexually abused, for instance, might feel cut off from their own bodies, unable to accept their own sexuality, or feel ugly and unattractive as physical beings. These people might need body image therapy to learn to accept and feel good about their bodies.

People with PTSD need to talk about and work through the trauma. Dissociation and flashbacks to the traumatic events are common problems for people with PTSD. They may injure themselves to stop the flashbacks or feel as if they are getting back in touch with reality. Talk therapy involves not only learning different ways of coping other than self-harm but also providing a safe place for the patient to remember the trauma, since it is often the case that traumatic details are not consciously remembered. The patient faces the bad memories, admits to himself or herself the fears and anger caused by the trauma, and is allowed to grieve about the past. Gradually, the traumatic events can be put in the past, and the person can appreciate being a survivor, learn to develop a positive self-image, and live in the present without being controlled by the need to avoid bad memories or the belief that he or she deserved whatever caused the trauma.

In all of these therapies, however, new skills for dealing with intense emotions are a part of the treatment. Walsh says that nine types of replacement skills—strategies to use instead of self-injury—may be helpful for people. They are:

1. *Negative replacement behaviors*
2. *Mindful breathing skills*
3. *Visualization techniques*
4. *Physical exercise*
5. *Writing*
6. *Artistic expression*
7. *Playing or listening to music*
8. *Communicating with others*
9. *Diversion [distraction] techniques*[51]

Mindfulness

Mindful breathing and visualization are two important coping skills. They are not distractions the way exercise, writing, and music are. They are to be used whether or not the person is thinking about self-injuring and are a way to practice reducing general stress in one's life. "Mindful breathing skills," Walsh said, "are often the most important in learning to give up self-injury."[52] Mindful breathing means concentrating on calm, relaxed breathing and not thinking about other things.

Walsh says that self-injurers are often so distressed that they are unable to focus and think clearly. They cannot let go of their negative emotions and are overwhelmed by them. Walsh teaches his clients to practice slow, deep, in-and-out breathing while they say something silently inside their minds such as "Letting go of x."[53] The x can be anything, such as anxiety, perfectionism, anger, fear, or guilt.

When people are focused, calm, and relaxed, they can practice visualizing—or clearly imagining—peaceful, happy scenes, such as lying on a beach or flying effortlessly through the sky like a bird. Visualization techniques like this are soothing and calming. The more calm and relaxed a person is, the less likely he or she is to feel the need to self-injure. Walsh practices visualization techniques with his patients during therapy sessions so that they can use these techniques on their own whenever they are feeling stress and emotional turmoil.

Mindful breathing and visualization can help a sufferer manage his or her emotions and stress as an alternative to self-harm.

Mimicry and Other Negative Replacements

Negative replacement behaviors are a completely different way of dealing with emotional turmoil. They are ways of mimicking or pretending to self-harm without actually doing it. For example, instead of cutting, the person might draw on the skin with a red marker. Other negative replacement behaviors include briefly applying an ice pack to the skin or stroking the skin with a soft brush and concentrating on the feeling. People can also draw a picture of the injury they want to perform or describe injuring themselves on a recording device. None of these activities actually damage the body, but they might feel real enough to satisfy the urge to self-injure. Walsh suggests negative replacement behaviors for some people early on in therapy, before healthier techniques have been learned, but they are controversial among many therapists. Conterio and Lader, for example, are firmly opposed to negative replacement behaviors. They argue that such techniques keep people focused on self-injury and preoccupied with hurting themselves. S.A.F.E. Alternatives forbids negative replacement behaviors in its program out of concern that they may increase the urge for actual self-injury.

Walsh agrees that negative replacement behaviors might "cue actual self-injury because [they] are so similar to the real thing."[54] However, he argues that the behaviors can help

One thing therapists commonly suggest is painting or drawing on the body when patients have the urge to self-harm.

some people to make the transition from self-injury to healthy replacement techniques. For example, Walsh tells the story of a client he calls Nikki. She would cut a grid of marks into her arms using an X-Acto knife. Her negative replacement behavior was to use the X-Acto knife to cut exactly the same pattern into layers of construction paper. She said that this activity helped her to avoid self-injury several times during the beginning of her therapy. Later, she learned healthier coping skills and dropped the negative replacement behavior.

How Helpful Is Medication?

While people are in therapy for self-injury and learning replacement skills, some professionals use medication to help clients control self-injury urges and focus on recovery. Although no medication has been developed to stop self-injury, certain psychological disorders can be eased with the appropriate medication. For example, a person who self-injures and suffers from depression might be prescribed an antidepressant. Antianxiety medication might be used for people with anxiety disorders. Medications can improve mood and increase motivation in therapy, but few studies have shown that they can reduce self-injury behaviors. Some clinicians share the philosophy that medications mask feelings and should be used as little as possible. They want patients to feel their emotions and learn to deal with them, rather than to ease the emotions with medication. Other experts believe that a combination of medication for psychological disorders and therapy works well for people who self-injure.

Some researchers have wondered whether self-injury is a physical addiction like alcoholism or drug addiction. With these addictions, drugs are sometimes used that can block the effects of the abused drugs. The theory is that if the addictive substance provides no reward or good feeling, the person will stop craving it. A drug that blocks the effects of opiates (such as heroin or morphine) on the brain is called an opiate blocking agent. One such drug, Naltrexone, has helped people recover from opiate addiction and has helped alcoholics. It also blocks endorphins, which are natural opiates produced by the brain. If self-injurers use their behavior to increase stress-soothing endorphins in their brains, perhaps opiate blockers could reduce self-injury episodes. Naltrexone has stopped self-injury in some people who harm themselves as a result of autism or intellectual disability, so researchers have studied Naltrexone with people who have BPD and also self-injure. The results have not been completely positive. Naltrexone and other opiate blockers have reduced self-injury in some people with BPD and other disorders, but have not changed behaviors at all in other studies. Research is still ongoing, but at present, no appropriate medication has been identified for self-injury addictions.

If psychiatrists do prescribe something, it is likely to be a drug that treats the underlying mental issue that caused the self-injury. However, the problem with this is that it is sometimes not immediately apparent which disorder a person has. For example, the symptoms of anxiety and depression can be very similar, so it is difficult to know which one a person has. He or she may even suffer from both at once, which adds to the difficulty of diagnosis and prescription.

Impact of Self-Help

Even though no perfect therapy or "magic pill" for self-injury exists, most people can and do recover with a combination of courage, determination, support from professionals, and self-help. On the Internet, for example, people turn to other self-injurers for understanding, encouragement, and tips for dealing with their self-harm behaviors. On websites dedicated to helping people who self-injure, members share personal stories, support each other, and report recovery successes to encourage others.

Psychologists Craig D. Murray and Jezz Fox of the University of Manchester in England conducted a study of one self-harm Internet discussion group in 2006. The researchers interviewed forum participants and concluded that the group helped many members to reduce the severity and frequency of their self-injury. It enabled people to make social connections, to feel understood, and to get emotional support at any time of the day or night that they needed help.

Internet support groups enable members to learn from each other how to help themselves. On the NSHN forum, for instance, participants may suggest distractions to try when the urge to self-injure is strong. What works for one person may not work for another, but everyone can see all the ideas and try a suggestion that seems appealing. Some of the contributed distraction suggestions have included "throwing socks against a wall," "ripping up paper into small pieces," "popping bubble wrap," "rubbing body lotion on where you want to hurt yourself," "organising your room, clothes, photographs," "playing with play dough or modelling clay," "watching a candle burn," and "dressing up, glamorous or silly."[55] The NSHN forum members work to break the self-destructive cycle of self-injury, whether or not they have real-world therapy or treatment. They are determined to help themselves.

Popping a balloon can be one healthy alternative to self-harm.

Light at the End of the Tunnel

Most people who self-injure do find the strength to end their self-destruction, although the process may take years. People may try several different treatments before they find the approach that works for them; they may successfully recover and then relapse during a period of stress and harm themselves again. However, with continued effort, a large majority find that the desire to self-injure does go away and that they have healed. Walsh said:

> My work with self-injurers has taught me, again and again, that great things are possible from those who are able to transform pain into affirmation. The life stories of self-injurers often move from anguish, isolation, and bodily harm to accomplishment, affiliation [positive relationships], and self-protection. We professionals are fortunate to play some role in assisting these seekers to find a higher ground.[56]

CHAPTER 5

Prevention Strategies

Faith Davis Johnson, an eighth-grade teacher in Dallas, Texas, wrote a newspaper article in May 2010 about the concerning increase in self-harm incidents in school-aged populations. Worried that adequate information and training was not being made available, she noticed that few schools in the country even had programs established to help fight the issue, either through prevention or intervention of self-injurious behaviors, even as the self-harm behaviors were just beginning to impact a student's life. Since there is a relatively high rate of self-harm in students, it is important for schools to be able to address the issue of self-harm in an effective way.

Johnson believed that schools should both be able to provide support and discuss prevention of self-injury, but she became frustrated as she saw a nationwide failure in schools to meet those minimal standards. Often, it is not that school personnel do not care, but rather that research is still being done on this issue. Johnson recommended that programs be put in place to train school staff on how to deal with students' NSSI. This would improve the chances of self-injuring students seeking help and make sure that they do get the proper help when they ask for it. Until such programs are used in all schools, there will continue to be a disastrous gap in the education system's ability to fully and accurately address the problem of self-injury.

Accurate Diagnosis, Prevention, and Risk Factors

Self-injury research experts and clinicians acknowledge that there is still debate over whether NSSI is a symptom of other disorders or a disorder in its own right, which also makes it difficult to identify all the causes and risk factors involved or predict which people might become addicted to self-injury. So how can they know which prevention efforts will work? According to the Cornell Research Program on Self-Injury and Recovery, "Although experienced therapists in this area can offer advice based on experience, few studies which actually test detection, intervention and treatment strategies have been conducted."[57] No one knows for sure how to prevent self-injury, but Cornell researchers, along with other experts, are trying to address the problem.

The Cornell researchers, as well as other researchers around the world, look at what is known about some of the reasons people begin to self-injure, and they consider the risk factors that might trigger self-injury experimentation. They consider such factors as psychological disorders, emotional distress, the role of the media, the spread of ideas and behaviors among groups of people, and the need for others to know what to do when someone begins to experiment with self-injury. Then they suggest several possible prevention strategies that might be useful.

School Interventions

Two of the strategies identified by the Cornell program include increasing "social connectedness" and paying attention to "stress in the external environment."[58] Social connectedness is about the support of family, friends, and school. Stresses in the external environment might include problems such as bullying at school or family problems at home. Instead of feeling socially connected, people who self-injure often report feelings of loneliness, isolation, and invisibility. Family problems may include abuse, neglect, or trauma, but they may also be stresses such as a divorce, a death in the family, or the chronic illness of a parent. Psychological reactions to stresses and lack of connectedness can lead to self-destructive behavior as a coping mechanism. Self-destructive behaviors are risky actions that may include eating disorders and substance abuse, which are common behaviors in people who self-injure, too.

Although no one knows how to predict who will turn to self-injury, experts do believe that supportive programs for people at risk could reduce all self-destructive behaviors. Because so many people who begin to self-injure are students, Cornell researchers and other experts suggest that school interventions aimed at helping students reach out to others and teaching healthy coping strategies could reduce self-injury in children and teens.

Increasing social connectedness may help decrease self-injurious behaviors.

Saving and Empowering Young Lives in Europe

In 2010, the European Union began a large, long-term research study to test the usefulness of different preventive methods for risk-taking and self-destructive behaviors. These behaviors include alcohol and drug use, self-injury, suicide attempts, aggression, depression, anxiety, and involvement in other dangerous situations. The project was named Saving and Empowering Young Lives in Europe (SEYLE). It involved 11,000 teens in schools in 11 different countries. In different schools, the researchers tested the value of three different kinds of interventions to reduce self-destructive behaviors. In some schools, the researchers provided "gatekeeper training" for teachers and school staff. This means school staff were trained to recognize students engaging in at-risk behavior. The teachers were taught how to ask questions about an individual student's behavior, persuade the individual to seek or accept help, and refer the student to an appropriate helper, such as a therapist, counselor, or hospital. School staff were provided with cards listing appropriate sources of help in the community.

In other schools, the researchers provided professional screening services to identify at-risk students. They gave questionnaires about lifestyle choices and psychological problems to all the students in the school. Then, students who tested as having mental health problems, self-destructive behaviors, or high risk-taking behaviors were interviewed by a psychologist to determine whether they needed intervention. Students with social problems (for instance, bullying or isolation) were encouraged to join a healthy lifestyle group, such as clubs or sports activities. Those with depression, anxiety, phobias, substance abuse, NSSI, or suicidal thoughts were referred for professional treatment.

In still other schools, researchers conducted awareness training for all students. The researchers explained, "The awareness intervention is designed to promote knowledge of mental health, healthy lifestyles, and behaviors among adolescents enrolled in the SEYLE project."[59] Every participating student was given a

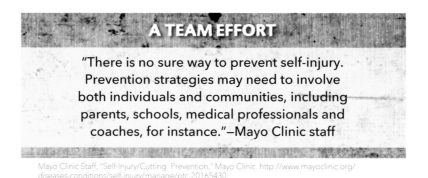

A TEAM EFFORT

"There is no sure way to prevent self-injury.
Prevention strategies may need to involve
both individuals and communities, including
parents, schools, medical professionals and
coaches, for instance."—Mayo Clinic staff

Mayo Clinic Staff, "Self-Injury/Cutting: Prevention," Mayo Clinic. http://www.mayoclinic.org/
diseases-conditions/self-injury/manage/ptc-20165430.

booklet that provided self-help advice and the names and phone numbers of counseling facilities and healthy lifestyle groups. Over a four-week period, the students learned about and discussed mental health issues, how to recognize depression and crisis and stress situations, and how to help a friend who is at risk. Posters about mental health and giving and accepting help were hung in each classroom. During discussion groups, the students were involved in role-playing sessions in which they acted out conflicts and explored healthy ways to resolve them. They practiced healthy coping skills when, for instance, they might be having a conflict with a teacher, parent, or friend. They explored how to react when they were under stress or during a crisis. The researchers hoped that these activities would help teens know what to do to resolve problems.

At the end of the SEYLE study in December 2011, the researchers began the process of reevaluating all the student participants to see what intervention worked best so those policies could be put in place in classrooms across Europe. A program called Youth Aware of Mental Health (YAM) was created using the study's findings. Students who attend this four-week program participate in role-play workshops to help them learn how to deal with issues that affect their mental health. The program is associated with a significant reduction of suicide attempts, anxiety, and depression. These findings underline the benefit of this universal suicide preventive intervention in schools.

Support Within the School System

In the United States, Matthew D. Selekman, a social worker and expert on self-injurers, believes that schools can help prevent self-injury with early identification of people who are just beginning to experiment with self-harm. Rather than including all the school's students in an educational and awareness program as SEYLE did, he suggests that school faculty can learn to "red-flag" or respond to clues that an individual student is experimenting with or thinking about self-injury. This approach is recommended by many experts who are concerned that whole-school educational programs might encourage contagion—the spread of self-harming behaviors from one person to another—or experimentation. Selekman says that teachers and others can be

Training teachers how to recognize and respond to early signs of self-injury can help students stop this risky behavior before too much harm is done.

taught to be alert for self-injury signs (such as wearing long-sleeved clothing in summer or displaying wounds) and then respond with compassion and an offer to help. He warns that too many adults react to signs of self-injury with "disgust, anxiety, or fear." School personnel have to be taught not to lecture or demand information; instead, they have to be "available for emotional connection, support, and advice when needed."[60]

Then, for at-risk students who are experimenting with self-harm, Selekman developed an intervention called the Stress-Busters' Leadership Group. This is a support group that teaches coping skills to teens who self-harm. The group is run by a counselor and assisted by students who have completed the program and want to help others. Selekman says, "Over nine sessions, students look at their strengths and 'protective shields'; learn skills related to mindfulness, meditation, loving kindness, and compassion toward self and others; focus on finding balance and harmony in their lives; learn how to navigate family minefields; and acquire effective tools for mastering school stress."[61]

Preventing the Epidemic

Selekman's approach to prevention targets individual at-risk students instead of the whole school population, in part because he believes that self-harming epidemics are a risk in schools. The Cornell researchers also believe that whole-school education about self-destructive behavior can backfire and encourage emotionally vulnerable teens to try the very behavior that educators are trying to reduce. They say that just teaching people about what self-injury is, why people do it, and how dangerous it is actually can cause an increase in experimenting with self-injury. Prevention of this kind of self-injury contagion is the goal of many experts who advise schools to avoid teaching about self-injury to everyone and to prevent self-injuring students from displaying their injuries to other students.

Walsh also suggests that schools have to have strategies in place to prevent self-injury from spreading among teens. He says that schools first have to identify the individual who is self-injuring and refer him or her to a specific "point person," such as the guidance counselor or school nurse. The point person then must explain to the self-injurer that it hurts their friends and other students to talk about self-injury. Self-injuring students should be encouraged to talk to point persons or therapists but asked not to talk about self-injuring to peers because such talk is "triggering" for vulnerable people. Also, based on recommendations from Walsh, the Cornell Research Program says, "Visible scars, wounds, and cuts should be discouraged."[62]

When to Seek Medical Help

LifeSigns, a British organization dedicated to helping people who self-injure, recognizes that sometimes prevention means avoiding danger and getting medical help. Its website advises:

It is very important that you tell someone if you have hurt yourself severely or if you have taken an overdose/ swallowed chemical substances. It is normal to be scared, but it is essential to get proper medical attention as quickly as possible. The following bullet points give some situations where medical attention should be sought; however it is not exhaustive.

- *If the wound continues to bleed heavily once you have [tried first aid], including bandaging;*
- *If the cut is deep and has exposed underlying muscle, this is dark red in colour and may look like a slab of meat;*
- *If you have lost sensation in the area of injury, or more widespread; you may have damaged a nerve;*
- *If a burn is on a sensitive area of the body (e.g., face), over a joint or on the palm—the healing process creates scar tissue that can shrink the skin, causing potential movement difficulties for life;*
- *If a burn is severe, or large in area;*
- *If a burn is caused by chemicals;*
- *If after a few hours or several days you can see the wound is infected; it could be red, sore, swollen or weeping.[1]*

1. LifeSigns.org, "First Aid for Self-Injury and Self-Harm." www.lifesigns.org.uk/ first-aid-for-self-injury-and-self-harm/.

Few scientific studies have been done to show whether or not contagion is real, but many educators and professionals assume from practical experience that self-injury is contagious and that prevention efforts should focus on contagion. Because of this "contagious quality," some experts do not approve of the idea of group counseling for self-injuring people. These experts argue that self-injurers can be involved in groups that teach coping skills or aim to improve self-esteem, but they should not discuss self-injury behaviors in the group. Such talk can trigger self-injury episodes in other group members.

The Importance of Peer Help

Despite concerns about contagion, self-injury professionals recognize that peers and friends are often the first people to know when someone begins to self-injure. Generally, friends and peers do not want to imitate the self-injurer; instead, they are worried, perhaps horrified, and desperately want to help. One approach to helping young people help someone who self-injures is called the Signs of Self-Injury Prevention Program. The program consists of an educational DVD and discussion kit designed for high school students that teaches how to recognize signs of self-injury and how to respond to an individual in need of help. It is based on a similar program for suicide prevention, called the Signs of Suicide (SOS) Prevention Program, developed by the nonprofit organization Screening for Mental Health. That program has been scientifically studied and shown to reduce suicide risk in young people.

The Signs of Self-Injury program teaches the ACT method of intervention to high school students. ACT stands for acknowledge, care, and tell. Acknowledge means that students learn to recognize the signs of self-destructive behavior instead of ignoring them, take the signs seriously, and are willing to listen to the person's feelings. Care is demonstrating concern and understanding, reassuring the self-injurer that he or she is not alone, and expressing worry for the friend or loved one who self-injures. Tell means to tell a responsible, trusted adult who can get the individual the help and treatment he or she needs. The Signs of Self-Injury Prevention Program can give friends the tools they need to help each other or allow a self-injurer to recognize what to do to help himself or herself. Experts hope that it will have the same positive effect of reducing self-injuring behavior in young people that the SOS program has had.

Media Highlights

Prevention of self-injury may depend on educating young people about the way the media can influence people's behavior, too. Cornell researchers theorize that news stories, songs, and celebrity talk about self-injury may be one cause of experimentation with self-injury, especially for teens. The researchers believe that helping adolescents and young adults pay attention to the messages the media sends them may reduce their risk of turning to glamorized but fundamentally poor coping strategies. Graphic news images of people's self-injuries can also be triggering for people who are fighting to avoid self-injury. Although no one is sure that teaching young people to reject the "fad" of self-injury can really prevent it, some researchers believe that some instances of self-injury might be prevented by school discussions of the effects of the media on society's view of what is "normal." The idea that the media can increase the incidence of self-injury is called "social contagion." It is not peers who trigger the contagion but the larger society.

Janis Whitlock explained, "Since the 1980s, references to NSSI in media stories and popular culture have risen sharply, and may be contributing to an increase in prevalence."[63] Studies of other kinds of self-destructive behavior have determined that the media affect what young people will try. Whitlock said:

Although we can never ... know whether media has influenced the spread of self-injurious behavior, many studies have shown that media [does] play a significant role in the spread of related behaviors such as suicidality, violence, and disordered eating ...

The Internet may be another vector for social contagion since it serves as a platform for hundreds of message boards, YouTube videos, and social networking sites where individuals with a history of or interest in self-injury provide informal support or share ideas.[64]

Staying Safe on the Internet

Caitlin Scafati was 14 years old when she began searching for sites on the Internet where she could find support for her self-injury and her eating disorder. Caitlin was overweight, teased at school, socially isolated, and depressed. She found sites on the Internet that encouraged her to starve herself into thinness and to cut herself to cope with her feelings of worthlessness and pain. Members on some discussion boards offered tips about cutting and talked about self-injury as just a lifestyle choice. Caitlin felt understood and accepted by the anonymous people on the boards. She read about celebrities who had admitted to injuring themselves, and these stories, she said, "made it seem cool and OK."[65] Unlike reputable self-injury sites that are dedicated to helping self-injurers, the sites Caitlin found harmed her and made cutting seem cool instead of an unhealthy way to cope. Fortunately, Caitlin told her parents about her self-injury when she was 15, and they got her into counseling.

Caitlin is an adult now and has recovered from both of her self-destructive behaviors. She knows the sites she visited were dangerous and has stayed away from them for many years. They taught her dependency on her self-destructive behavior and did nothing, in the end, for her emotional pain.

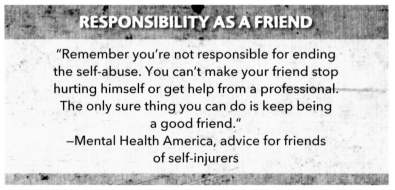

RESPONSIBILITY AS A FRIEND

"Remember you're not responsible for ending the self-abuse. You can't make your friend stop hurting himself or get help from a professional. The only sure thing you can do is keep being a good friend."
—Mental Health America, advice for friends of self-injurers

Mental Health America, "Factsheet: Self-Injury." www.nmha.org/go/information/get-info/self-injury.

In the United Kingdom, Oxford University researchers did a study of young people who self-injure and discovered that one out of five had first learned about the behavior online. For

A Cry for Help

In interviews, Angelina Jolie has been open about injuring herself as a teen, but she is upset that some interviewers have made it seem as if her self-injury is something to admire or imitate. She explained, "I was just ... a kid. I was like 13. And, I was saying that it is not something that is cool. It's not cool. And I understand that it is a cry for help."[1] Jolie does not self-injure now and does not encourage others to do it, but she remembers what happened after one interviewer wrote a story that made her self-injury seem interesting:

> And then I met somebody who said they'd seen movies of mine and then showed me where they had cut themselves. I had to explain, first off, not to do that. But it made me really ... angry at the people who represent me in a way that would get that person to do that and show me. I don't understand why people would want to use something so damaging. It's like, let's make me look "cool" and worry a lot of people in my family.[2]

1. Quoted in "Why Some of Us Self Harm," Lady in the Purple Hijab, May 10, 2016. theladyinthe-purplehijab.wordpress.com/tag/angelina-jolie/.

2. Quoted in "Why Some of Us Self Harm."

Angelina Jolie has harmed herself in the past but tells people that it is not something to admire or imitate.

example, 17-year-old Danielle, of Belfast, Ireland, said, "I think the Internet played a major role; I think it started off my self-harm. I was already thinking about it so [I] went to the web to find out more. I just typed 'self-harm' and there were hundreds of videos. Some are good but others can be very damaging. If I see a picture [of cuts], it can encourage me to do it."[66]

The British Royal College of Psychiatrists urged in 2010 that all websites should remove any material that might trigger self-harm. It said that too many sites glorify or glamorize self-injury. Sites such as YouTube have many thousands of videos about self-harm and cutting. British psychiatrist Margaret Murphy explained, "The kinds of things we are worried about are the graphic videos of self-harm [injuries] that are posted to sites like YouTube. Young people tell us that images can trigger memories and that makes them much more likely to self-harm."[67] The British doctors have asked all website owners to link directly to websites that offer professional help on pages where videos or discussions of self-injury encourage the behavior.

YouTube does take down any self-injury videos that frankly urge other young people to self-injure, but, like other Internet sites, it does not forbid all videos of self-harm. The idea is that people should be free to discuss issues and post videos that are honest communications about social problems. Although banning material about self-injury from the Internet might prevent some instances of repetitive self-injury, Google, the owner of YouTube, says that it must maintain a balance between safety and free speech.

Some users report that seeking out self-harm materials has actually helped them. Sites such as Tumblr and Instagram try to shut down hashtags that include the word self-harm, but users create new ones that are harder to find and do not directly reference self-injury—for example, #blithe or #ehtilb ("blithe" spelled backwards). Some people who use these hashtags to find other self-injurers report that the people they have connected with online have become a close-knit community, offering the emotional support and understanding they may not feel they are getting from non-injurers. However, some experts fear that people may use these relationships as a replacement for real therapy, which can stop them from learning better coping mechanisms. Additionally, researchers worry that the self-harm photos people find on Instagram, either accidentally or on purpose, will be triggering.

In the end, avoiding material that triggers self-harm or experimentation is up to each individual. Whitlock, Conterio, and Lader suggest that clinicians explore with their clients whether they should avoid Internet use that could trigger or encourage self-injury. The Mayo Clinic believes school education about the possible negative influence of media might reduce the risks of experimentation for all young people. The Royal College of Psychiatrists has called for better training for teachers about the problem and dangers of self-injury so they can learn to deal effectively with students who experiment with hurting themselves or have become addicted to the behavior. Former self-injurers recommend that other young people stay away from any Internet material that makes self-injury seem acceptable or that triggers the urge to self-harm. However, individuals who find themselves drawn to self-injury cannot be completely protected by avoiding media representations of the behavior. True prevention of self-injury is about each troubled individual and means, Lader says, "dealing with the real issue—their out-of-control emotions."[68]

Prevention Is Key

If there is anything to be learned from all of the research and studies about self-injury, it is this: prevention is key. For sufferers, the biggest concern is stopping the self-injurious behavior before it occurs or prevent it from happening again. Unfortunately, experts are still weighing in on how to prevent self-injury. What they do know is that it is impossible to control society's messages completely, so the focus is more on how former self-injurers can avoid being triggered.

In response to the growing epidemic, many blogs and websites have attempted to combat the situation through offerings of affirmations and caring, positive messages to anyone who may be considering self-injury as a coping mechanism. For someone considering self-injury, these affirmations may be useful in destructive behavior prevention. Some examples include "My feelings are real and important and need to be listened to," "When I feel bad or guilty or dirty, that's how I have been made to feel by things that have happened in my life. It's not the truth about me," and "I have suffered more than enough in my life. I can have some kindness now. I don't deserve to be hurt anymore."[69]

Still others find different ways to cope instead of resorting to self-harm. For instance, one woman described how her therapist recommended drawing something beautiful on the area where she would consider self-injuring. Her legs covered in intricate swirls, she found beauty in her pain without self-injury.

Some former self-injurers use tattoos to cover their old scars or remind themselves of their inner strength.

Life After Self-Harm

Even after receiving help, many self-injurers struggle. Seeing photos of scars or reading stories about other people self-harming can trigger a relapse, or return to self-injury. This often feels like failure and triggers more negative emotions that lead to more self-harm. However, relapse is not failure and does not mean that recovery is impossible; rather, it is a normal part of recovery. Recovery is a long and challenging process, and for some people, it may never be truly finished. An important part of the process is learning which triggers to avoid in order to prevent a relapse.

Scars remain on the body long after the person stops self-injuring. Some former self-injurers do not like to see them because the scars remind them of a difficult time in their life, so they cover them up with long sleeves, bracelets, or tattoos. Others see them as a reminder of how far they have come, so they do not cover them. Those who choose not to hide their scars may encounter strangers who want to know how they got their scars. This can be very uncomfortable for recovering self-injurers to talk about. The Cornell Research Program on Self-Injury and Recovery offers these tips:

> It is not your responsibility to satisfy someone else's curiosity. There are ways of talking about your experience that allow you to be both honest and kind without going into [too] much detail. Here are some examples:
>
> - "Thanks for asking, but it is not something I talk about with people I do not know well."
>
> - "These are scars from a hard time in my life, but I am not comfortable talking about it now."
>
> - "Yes, they are noticeable, aren't they? That is a story for another time and place."[70]

In addition to therapy, taking care of the body is an important step on the road to recovery. This includes getting enough sleep, eating healthy meals, and regularly getting a moderate amount of exercise. A strong support system is also helpful; if a person does not have friends or family to rely on, they can join a local support group or a club that lets them meet new people. Recovery from self-harm may seem like an impossible or unwelcome task sometimes, but the end result—a happier, healthier life—is well worth the effort.

Introduction: A Growing Epidemic

1. Self Injury Foundation, "Mission." www.selfinjuryfoundation.org.

2. Quoted in Laura A. Dorko, "Literature Review: Development of a Website for Educators Addressing How to Understand, Recognize, and Respond to Student Self-Injury," Educators and Self-Injury, 2009. educatorsandselfinjury.com/literature-review.

3. Deb Martinson, "Self-Help: Organized and Otherwise," ihurtmyselftoday.com. ihurtmyselftoday.com/self-help-organized-and-otherwise.

Chapter 1: Intentional Personal Harm

4. Quoted in Elizabeth E. Lloyd-Richardson, Matthew K. Nock, and Mitchell J. Prinstein, "Chapter 3: Functions of Adolescent Nonsuicidal Self-Injury," in Mary K. Nixon and Nancy L. Heath, eds., *Self-Injury in Youth: The Essential Guide to Assessment and Intervention.* New York, NY: Routledge, 2009, p. 30.

5. Quoted in Lloyd-Richardson, et al., *Self-Injury in Youth*, p. 31.

6. Quoted in Karen Conterio and Wendy Lader, *Bodily Harm: The Breakthrough Healing Program for Self-Injurers.* New York, NY: Hyperion, 1998, p. 134.

7.   Mary K. Nixon and Nancy L. Heath, "Introduction to Nonsuicidal Self-Injury in Adolescence," in *Self-Injury in Youth: The Essential Guide to Assessment and Intervention*, p. 4.

8.   Elana Premack Sandler, "Self-Injury: Addiction? Parasuicide? Cry for Help? Or None of the Above?" *Psychology Today*, July 2, 2009. www.psychologytoday.com/blog/promoting-hope-preventing-suicide/200907/self-injury-addiction-para suicide-cry-help-or-none-the.

9.   Tracy Alderman, "Tattoos and Piercings: Self-Injury?" *Psychology Today*, December 10, 2009. www.psychologytoday.com/blog/the-scarred-soul/200912/tattoos-and-piercings-self-injury.

10. Dr. Helen Okoye, "Nonsuicidal Self-Injury DSM-5," Theravive. www.theravive.com/therapedia/Nonsuicidal-Self--Injury-DSM--5.

11. Shirah Vollmer, MD, "NSSID," *Shirah Vollmer MD*, May 12, 2016. shirahvollmermd.wordpress.com/2016/05/12/nssid.

12. Patrick L. Kerr, Jennifer J. Muehlenkamp, and James M. Turner, "Nonsuicidal Self-Injury: A Review of Current Research for Family Medicine and Primary Care Physicians," *Journal of the American Board of Family Medicine*, vol. 23, no. 2, 2010, pp. 240–59. www.jabfm.com/cgi/content/full/23/2/240.

13. Quoted in "True Extent of Self-Harm Amongst Teenagers Revealed," *Science Daily*, September 4, 2008. www.sciencedaily.com/releases/2008/09/080903101414.htm.

14. Michael Eddleston, M.H. Rezvi Sheriff, and Keith Hawton, "Deliberate Self Harm in Sri Lanka: An Overlooked Tragedy in the Developing World," *British Medical Journal*, vol. 317, July 11, 1998, pp. 133–35. www.ncbi.nlm.nih.gov/pmc/articles/PMC1113497/.

Chapter 2: Reasons for Self-Injury

15. Quoted in Conterio and Lader, *Bodily Harm*, p. 61.

16. Quoted in Conterio and Lader, *Bodily Harm*, p. 61.

17. Quoted in Conterio and Lader, *Bodily Harm*, p. 63.

18. Quoted in Conterio and Lader, *Bodily Harm*, pp. 67–68.

19. Quoted in Conterio and Lader, *Bodily Harm*, p. 82.

20. Quoted in Conterio and Lader, *Bodily Harm*, p. 78.

21. Digby Tantam and Nick Huband, *Understanding Repeated Self-Injury*. New York, NY: Palgrave Macmillan, 2009, p. 96.

22. Tantam and Huband, *Understanding Repeated Self-Injury*, p. 32.

23. Matthew K. Nock, "Self-Injury," *Annual Review of Clinical Psychology*, vol. 6, 2010, p. 351. www.annualreviews.org/doi/abs/10.1146/annurev.clinpsy.121208.131258.

24. Tracy Alderman, "Myths and Misconceptions of Self-Injury: Part II," *Psychology Today*, October 22, 2009. www.psychologytoday.com/blog/the-scarred-soul/200910/myths-and-misconceptions-self-injury-part-ii.

25. Justin Mills, "The Art of Bloodletting," Personal Stories, Psyke. www.psyke.org/articles/en/art.

26. Parent Information on Self-Injury/Cutting Behavior. www.northcolonie.org/wp-content/uploads/2015/06/SJHS_guidance_self_injury_information.pdf.

27. Janis L. Whitlock, Jane L. Powers, and John Eckenrode, "The Virtual Cutting Edge: The Internet and Adolescent Self-Injury," *Developmental Psychology*, vol. 42, no.3, 2006. www.apa.org/pubs/journals/releases/dev-423407.pdf.

28. Nock, "Self-Injury," p. 356.

Chapter 3: Inherent Risks of Self-Injury

29. Conterio and Lader, *Bodily Harm*, pp. 228–35.

30. Barent W. Walsh, *Treating Self-Injury: A Practical Guide*. New York, NY: Guilford, 2008, p. 22.

31. "Self-Injury," *Nursing Times*, February 23, 2009. www.nursingtimes.net/whats-new-in-nursing/self-injury/1995882.article.

32. Jennifer, "My Trip to the E.R.," Personal Stories, Psyke. www.psyke.org/personal/j/jennifer.

33. Conterio and Lader, *Bodily Harm*, p. 228.

34. "Self Injury FAQ," Psyke. www.psyke.org/faqs.

35. Deb Martinson, "Self-Injury: You Are NOT the Only One," Buslist. buslist.org/injury.html.

36. "Talking About Self-Injury with Others," SelfInjury.net. self-injury.net/information-recovery/recovery/talking-about-self-injury-others.

37. Charlotte, "Untitled," Personal Stories, Psyke. www.psyke.org/personal/c/charlotte.

38. Conterio and Lader, *Bodily Harm*, p. 229.

39. Quoted in Anthony Burt, "Telling Someone You Self-Harm," The Mix, December 23, 2015. www.themix.org.uk/mental-health/self-harm/telling-someone-you-self-harm-5682.html.

40. Quoted in Anthony Burt, "Telling Someone You Self-Harm."

41. Tracy Alderman, "Helping Those Who Hurt Themselves," *Prevention Researcher*, vol. 7, no. 4, 2000, pp. 5–8. www.cyc-net.org/reference/refs-self-mutilation-alderman1.html.

Chapter 4: The Recovery Process

42. Conterio and Lader, *Bodily Harm*, p. 295.

43. Tracy Alderman, interview by Bob McMillan, "Self-Injury," transcript from online Concerned Counseling conference, March 3, 1998. www.cyc-net.org/reference/refs-self-mutilation-alderman2.html.

44. Mills, "The Art of Bloodletting." ct.counseling.org/2014/10/responding-to-the-rise-in-self-injury-among-youth.

45. "Cognitive Behavioral Therapy," Good Therapy, July 2, 2015. www.goodtherapy.org/learn-about-therapy/types/cognitive-behavioral-therapy.

46. Brent G. Richardson and Kendra A. Surmitis, "Responding to the Rise in Self-Injury Among Youth," *Counseling Today*, October 23, 2014.

47. "An Overview of Dialectical Behavior Therapy," Psych Central, 2016. psychcentral.com/lib/an-overview-of-dialectical-behavior-therapy.

48. Walsh, *Treating Self-Injury: A Practical Guide*, p. 121.

49. Stacey Freedenthal, PhD, "The Use of No-Suicide Contracts," Speaking of Suicide, 2013. www.speakingofsuicide.com/2013/05/15/no-suicide-contracts.

50. Walsh, *Treating Self-Injury: A Practical Guide*, p. 122.

51. Walsh, *Treating Self-Injury: A Practical Guide*, p. 127.

52. Walsh, *Treating Self-Injury: A Practical Guide*, p. 129.

53. Walsh, *Treating Self-Injury: A Practical Guide*, p. 134.

54. Walsh, *Treating Self-Injury: A Practical Guide*, p. 129.

55. NSHN Forum, "Distractions That Can Help,"

National Self Harm Network. www.nshn.co.uk/forum/index.php?topic=16069.0.

56. Walsh, *Treating Self-Injury: A Practical Guide*, p. 274.

Chapter 5: Prevention Strategies

57. "About Self-Injury and Recovery: Detection, Intervention, and Treatment," The Cornell Research Program on Self-Injury and Recovery, 2016. www.selfinjury.bctr.cornell.edu/about-self-injury.html.

58. "About Self-Injury and Recovery: Prevention," The Cornell Research Program on Self-Injury and Recovery.

59. Danuta Wasserman, et al., "Saving and Empowering Young Lives in Europe (SEYLE): A Randomized Controlled Trial," *BMC Public Health 2010*, vol. 10, no. 192, April 13, 2010. www.biomedcentral.com/1471-2458/10/192.

60. Matthew D. Selekman, "Helping Self-Harming Students," *Health and Learning*, vol. 67, no. 4, December 2009/January 2010, pp. 48–53. www.ascd.org/publications/educational_leadership/dec09/vol67/num04/Helping_Self-Harming_Students.aspx.

61. Selekman, "Helping Self-Harming Students."

62. Kate Bubrick, Jaclyn Goodman, and Janis Whitlock, "Non-Suicidal Self-Injury in Schools: Developing and Implementing School Protocol," The Cornell Research Program on Self-Injury and Recovery, 2010. www.selfinjury.bctr.cornell.edu/documents/schools.pdf.

63. Janis Whitlock, "The Cutting Edge: Non-Suicidal Self-Injury in Adolescence," Research Facts and Findings, ACT for Youth Center of Excellence: A Collaboration of Cornell University, University of Rochester, and New York State Center for School Safety, p. 4. www.actforyouth.net/documents/NSSI_Dec09.pdf.

64. Whitlock, "The Cutting Edge."

65. Quoted in Mary Fischer, "Thrills That Kill," *Readers Digest*, February 2006. www.gaoglish.cn/reading/g1/20080920141943_2.pdf.

66. Quoted in "Young People Self-Harming with Sharp Objects Up 50%," BBC Radio 1 Newsbeat, March 12, 2010. www.bbc.co.uk/newsbeat.

67. Quoted in "Young People Self-Harming with Sharp Objects Up 50%."

68. Quoted in Fischer, "Thrills That Kill."

69. "Affirmations for People Who Self-Harm," Psyke, 2002, reprint from *Self-Harm Overcome by Understanding and Tolerance (SHOUT)*. www.psyke.org/history/200210/coping/affirmations.

70. Patricia Rothenberg and Janis Whitlock, "Wounds Heal but Scars Remain: Responding When Someone Notices and Asks About Your Past Self-Injury," The Cornell Research Program on Self-Injury and Recovery, 2013. www.selfinjury.bctr.cornell.edu/perch/resources/wounds-heal-pm-4.pdf.

DISCUSSION QUESTIONS

Chapter 1: Intentional Personal Harm

1. Do you think NSSI is a symptom of a psychological disorder, or should it be considered a diagnosis in itself?

2. Do you think going to therapy is seen as a bad thing? If so, how can you help change that view?

3. If you bite your nails or pick at a scab, is that self-injury? Why or why not?

Chapter 2: Reasons for Self-Injury

1. What are some of the emotional reasons that people turn to repetitive self-injury?

2. How is self-injury like drug addiction?

3. What life experiences might make someone with good, loving parents feel powerless and uncared for?

Chapter 3: Inherent Risks of Self-Injury

1. What types of physical risks can occur with self-injury?

2. What are some emotional risks of self-injury?

3. What are some of the reactions that family and friends tend to go through when they find out a person is self-injuring?

Chapter 4: The Recovery Process

1. Provide arguments for and against self-harm contracts and their usefulness in prevention and treatment.

2. Which treatment methods do you think would be most successful in helping self-injurers recover?

3. What distraction or skill do you think might best help a person avoid self-injuring?

Chapter 5: Prevention Strategies

1. Do you think self-injury is a problem in your school?
Should the school be addressing the issue?
Why or why not?

2. Do you believe self-injury is contagious? Why or why not?

3. If a friend or loved one admitted to you that he or she has been self-injuring, what should you say or do? Would it be easy or hard to respond with compassion and calm?

Mental Health America
500 Montgomery Street
Suite 820
Alexandria, VA 22314
Phone: (703) 684-7722
Toll-free: (800) 969-6642
Website: www.mentalhealthamerica.net
This organization's mission is to educate the public about mental health, fight for equal and appropriate mental health care for all people, and provide support to people living with mental health issues or substance abuse problems.

National Alliance on Mental Illness (NAMI)
3803 N. Fairfax Drive
Suite 100
Arlington, VA 22203
Phone: (703) 524-7600
Helpline: (800) 950-6264
Website: www.nami.org
NAMI is a national nonprofit outreach, educational, and advocacy organization dedicated to improving the lives of people with mental illnesses and their families.

7 Cups of Tea
Website: www.7cups.com
Using the app or the website, people can reach out to an anonymous listener to discuss problems big and small. The listener does not judge, solve problems, or give advice; the listener affirms emotions and gives users a safe place to vent their feelings. There are also peer chat rooms and resources that help people find a licensed therapist, either online or in their area.

To Write Love on Her Arms (TWLOHA)
TWLOHA, Inc.
P.O. Box 2203
Melbourne, FL 32902
Phone: (321) 499-3901
Website: twloha.com
To Write Love on Her Arms is a nonprofit organization that supports people suffering from depression, self-harm, and suicidal thoughts. The group sells merchandise so that the proceeds can be donated to recovery programs and research on how best to help people struggling with these issues. The website includes information on how people can get involved with TWLOHA in their communities.

Books

Bradshaw, Cheryl. *How to Like Yourself: A Teen's Guide to Quieting Your Inner Critic & Building Lasting Self-Esteem.* Oakland, CA: Instant Help Books, 2016.
High self-esteem can eliminate several of the risk factors for self-harm, but it can be difficult for people who do not think much of themselves to change their perception on their own. With humor and sincerity, Bradshaw discusses ways teens can improve their self-esteem.

Gratz, Kim L., and Alexander L. Chapman. *Freedom from Self-Harm: Overcoming Self-Injury with Skills from DBT and Other Treatments.* Oakland, CA: New Harbinger Productions, Inc, 2009.
This book dispels myths about self-injury; lists easy, healthy ways to manage stress; and gives advice on how to find the right therapist.

Guest, Jennifer. *The CBT Art Activity Book: 100 Illustrated Handouts for Creative Therapeutic Work.* Philadelphia, PA: Jessica Kingsley Publishers, 2016.
Combining art therapy and cognitive behavioral therapy, this workbook contains pages with coloring designs as well as space for people to journal about ways to change their thought patterns from negative to positive.

Roza, Greg. *Cutting and Self-Injury.* New York, NY: Rosen Publishing, 2014.
This volume explores the reasons why people self-injure, offers advice to them as well as their loved ones, and discusses treatment options.

Shapiro, Lawrence. *Stopping the Pain: A Workbook for Teens Who Cut and Self Injure*. Oakland, CA: Instant Help Books, 2008. Writing exercises help young adults think through their issues and put them into words in order to better understand themselves and the reasons for their self-injury. By doing these exercises, teens will identify the underlying emotional issues that cause them to harm themselves and learn healthier coping skills.

Websites

Befrienders Worldwide
www.befrienders.org
This international website offers support in 39 countries to people who are depressed, lonely, or despairing, with the goal of decreasing the risk of suicide by providing someone to listen. Support is offered by e-mail or hotlines. Most are available 24 hours a day.

The Mix
www.themix.org.uk
This United Kingdom-based website offers information about a variety of topics that affect young adults, including self-harm. A confidential live chat is available from 4:00 p.m. to 4:00 a.m. for people who need to talk to someone neutral about the problems they are experiencing.

Reach Out
us.reachout.com
Information and resources validated by health professionals are presented alongside tips and advice from students who have experienced mental health issues themselves. It includes advice for people who want to help a self-injuring loved one, forums where people can connect with others, and toll-free helplines for those who need immediate help.

Recover Your Life

www.recoveryourlife.com

One of the largest virtual support communities for self-injury on the Internet, Recover Your Life offers chat rooms, live help, a discussion forum, and advice for people who self-injure. It is a strong pro-recovery site.

Students Against Depression

studentsagainstdepression.org

Mental health professionals and fellow depression sufferers offer tips on how to deal with stress, depression, self-harm, and suicidal thoughts.

INDEX

ABOUT THE AUTHOR

Stephanie Mialki holds a BA in journalism and mass communication from St. Bonaventure University. She is an entrepreneur and a mother of two boys. She has a passion for helping business owners expand their businesses and markets and is a guru of digital marketing.